TERRAPSYCHOLOGY

TERRAPSYCHOLOGY

Re-engaging the Soul of Place

Craig Chalquist

Spring Journal Books
New Orleans, Louisiana

Published by
Spring Journal, Inc.;
627 Ursulines Street #7
New Orleans, Louisiana 70116
Tel.: (504) 524-5117
Fax: (504) 558-0088
Website: www.springjournalandbooks.com

Cover design by
Northern Cartographic
4050 Williston Road
South Burlington, VT 05403

Cover art designed by
Jane Allison Circle

Terrapsychology monogram designed by
Michael Mendis
24 Blackfriars Street
London, Ont. N6H 1K6
Canada

Printed in Canada
Text printed on acid-free paper

Library of Congress Cataloging-in-Publication Data Pending

DEDICATION

For Earth:
home, source of hope, destroyer, creator,
mother of the ancestors,
birther of myth.

Contents

CONTENTS

Acknowledgments

To Mary Watkins, Elizabeth Nelson, and Chellis Glendinning I owe two debts of gratitude: for serving on my dissertation committee at Pacifica Graduate Institute, and for mentoring me as I struggled to create concepts to describe and define five years of difficult qualitative research.

My editor, Nancy Cater, supported this book from the start, and with the patience of Sisyphus, despite the original manuscript's claylike stubbornness. From Daniel Graham and Linda Buzzell-Saltzman I received not only camaraderie combined with perceptive questioning and unfailing enthusiasm, but a constant, affirming presentness I knew I could rely on even when I did not need to.

My friend and colleague Laura Mitchell told me about her explorations in the hills near Escondido, California among the petroglyphs she wrote about in her doctoral dissertation. Her deeply felt sensitivity to that locale and to the San Diegan landscape that birthed us increased my appreciation for the vitality and intelligence of place, as has the richly stratified sensibility of the nomadic and poetic Matthew Cochran. I look forward to seeing both of them publish their extraordinary work.

My thanks go out to the graduate students at JFK University, Sonoma State, and Pacifica Graduate Institute for lively discussions that helped clarify the work.

Finally, I look forward to the day when this salute will not seem abnormal: *To all the places that appear in this book: You are my research partners in every sense that counts. Thank you for mentoring me, your student.*

—Craig Chalquist

Foreword

An oft-quoted statement by Albert Einstein says: "The significant problems we face cannot be solved at the same level of thinking we were at when we created them." As the magnitude of our ecological troubles is becoming ever more known, with issues such as global warming, peak oil, and environmental racism increasingly part of our awareness and our conversations, Einstein's words become a challenge to reach beyond our collective blind spots to find deeper wisdom.

No aspect of the environmental crisis speaks more compellingly than the current extinction spasm, a human-induced die-off that rivals the four great extinction events of prehistory. Noted biologist E. O. Wilson estimates that approximately 74 species per day are currently going extinct, and Michael Soule, one of the founders of conservation biology, suggests that what is at stake goes beyond the loss of individual species to the future evolutionary potential of those species that survive—their ability to adapt to changing conditions and ultimately to give rise to new species.

Through the work of the environmental movement and dedicated scientists, many people are beginning to awaken to the reality and magnitude of the extinction crisis. But at the same time, much of the general public remains uninformed, and the institutions that hold power in society—governments, corporations, and the like—are generally unconcerned or actively resistant to change. While environmental activists engage in much-needed "holding actions" to slow down the destruction, we still lack a comprehensive sense of how to live sustainably as a global community. We are increasingly aware of the need for something more, a source of knowledge that will guide us in addressing the extinction crisis and other environmental imbalances at their root, a perspective that originates from a place of wholeness and that can guide us back into balance.

In *Terrapsychology,* Craig Chalquist outlines a process for accessing such knowledge. His work is grounded in a profound observation of human relationships: there is a kind of magic that happens when one is seen with reverence and appreciation. The compassionate presence of another allows hidden dimensions of ourselves to emerge. This insight has formed the basis of countless human traditions of healing, from nature-based rites of passage to Buddhist wisdom to Western psychotherapy and humanistic psychology.

Terrapsychology takes this process beyond the human realm, even beyond what is conventionally considered alive, and into matter itself, organic and inorganic. Craig Chalquist lays out a process of listening—to the land, to specific locations, whether wilderness or city, to matter itself—to hear its needs, its pain, its wholeness, its perspective.

Indigenous, earth-based people through the ages have cultivated the ability to attend to the land with an awareness that is attuned to nuance, to subtle shifts in mood and atmosphere. This capacity has largely been lost to people of the modern world. The rationality of modern consciousness overrides our deeper sensitivities, much as the bright glare of the sun blocks our perception of the intricate patterns of starlight. *Terrapsychology* meets us where we are: several centuries into a mechanistic scientific worldview that has succeeded brilliantly in unearthing new information and manipulating nature, but has left us bereft of guidance regarding how to live. From this starting point, Craig Chalquist maps a path back into intimacy that is profound and visionary, yet specific and clear in its method. Through a series of practices such as placehosting, psychocartography, and archetypal geography, Chalquist guides us into dialogue with the land—sacred land, healthy land, suffering and neglected land.

I see two ways that this work can help us address the extinction crisis and other aspects of ecological imbalance. First, as the practices and perspective of *Terrapsychology* cultivate sensitivity to the psyche of the land, they will nurture in practitioners both the commitment to living in balance and the knowledge of how to do so. Second, and more challenging to our usual modes of thought, *Terrapsychology* presents the possibility of moving beyond our collective blind spots by asking the land itself what it needs, listening to the voices of endangered and even extinct species, inviting these non-ordinary sources of wisdom into dialogue with us. *Terrapsychology* challenges us to be humble enough to see that our rationality, a great gift when used appropriately, is by itself insufficient to the task before us.

Our ability to listen to the land isn't gone, it is simply dormant. Every human being alive today, no matter how alienated and disconnected, has descended from thousands of generations of indigenous ancestors, people whose survival depended on a keen attunement to natural cycles. The capacity to live in intimate communication with the more-than-human world is a part of our evolved psyche that may be muted, but never destroyed. *Terrapsychology* re-awakens this ability in a contemporary form, opening once again the ancient pathways between human minds and the voice of the Earth.

—Mary Gomes

I learn that the writer's pen is a microphone held up to the mouths of ancestors and even stones of long ago. … The magic of this is not so much in the power of the microphone as in the ability of the nonhuman object or animal to *be* and the human animal to *perceive its being*.

— Alice Walker

Summoned by the Voice of Place

> I walk out; I see something, some event that would otherwise have been utterly missed and lost; or something sees me, some enormous power brushes me with its clean wing, and I resound like a beaten bell.
>
> — Annie Dillard, *A Pilgrim at Tinker Creek*

Six years ago you could have found me under the glassy spires of downtown San Diego, the city of my birth, interviewing street artists, meeting with community activists in search of funding, and holding free psychology classes for parents on welfare. For my first year of doctoral fieldwork at Pacifica Graduate Institute I had been advised to reacquaint myself with the margins, the edges, the shadows of my hometown while monitoring my moods and dreams for clues about its psychic underside. "From out of the consulting room and into the world," read my psychological brief to myself.

With the growing sense I was overlooking something important, a depression moved in like fog along the coast. It was not the fieldwork; I had undertaken similar activities previously. I was depressed because of a relationship, or so I thought, but I did not understand why. The surface harmony in which my partner and I talked and listened to each other was strained again and again by a caginess, a guardedness, that continually marched back and forth in the psychological demilitarized zone between us, like a frontier soldier on patrol. No amount of probing for unanalyzed trauma or unconscious motivations healed it. From my end it felt like being haunted by a demon whose names might have been Defense, Fortification, Outpost, Citadel. Reaching out came to feel more and more like daring some risky border crossing.

Meanwhile, "Something is missing," I kept thinking as I wrote up my fieldwork for school. While conducting it I had toured the Gaslamp, traversed the Silver Gate, picked up sand dollars from the shoreline near the Del, spoken with artists and street people. I had stood under a statue of Cabrillo and looked out of a summer day onto endless sheets of shimmering blue on either side of North Island. I knew the wet touch of fool's gold at La Jolla Shores, the cold sting of seawater pounding the cliffs there, the moist snuffle of a giraffe eating from my hand at the Wild Animal Park in Escondido. San Diego, named for the flagship of Captain Vizcaino, who in turn was named after a saint who fought to protect a militarized border: my home, even though I chose to ignore the top gunners' jets screaming over Miramar, the aircraft carriers in the bay, the congested traffic, the smog, the flag-waving, squads of young Marines on leave, submarines at Point Loma, the SEALs, and Camp Pendleton, where the Border Patrol remained on the lookout just above the base for unwanted migrants surfacing from the south.

Two weeks after my relationship finally imploded from excessive guardedness, a feminine figure visited me one night in a dream. Thinking she was my former lover, I called her by name. But, *No*, she shook her head; and as I stared, I began to see that indeed the figure before me was not the woman I had loved. *That is not my name*, confirmed her look and the frown. I knew that frown, and the gloomy sense of presence she exuded, but somehow could not place them.

Then who are you? I asked her.

San Diego, she said, with a look the color of battleship steel. *My name is San Diego.*

I woke in shock, the cartographic image of a downward-turning bay clear in my mind's eye and a question to which I had no answer forming in my heart:

How could a place self-personify and speak to me from inside a dream?

———

For most psychological schools and perspectives that take dreams seriously, dream figures function as symbols of various aspects of the dreamer's mind, body, or immediate situation. A Freudian analyst hearing my dream might inquire about a mother problem, and a Jungian traditionalist might wonder about the state of my *anima*, the feminine side of a man, or his "woman within." Other analysts might investigate split-off fragments—"introjects"—of internalized "good mom" and "bad mom" impressions stored up over time, or, at a more transpersonal level, look keenly for the mythological Great Mother archetype. (By now the reader might well wonder whether psychotherapy sometimes finds *itself* saddled with a mother problem.) A medical doctor might ask what I had for dinner, a psychiatrist which medication might be most effective in silencing that figure whose deeply frowning mouth recalled the San Diego Bay. Few would be the experts willing to risk taking the dream figure at her word—staying *with* her, as the more daring of phenomenologists would recommend—even after the usual explanations I tried on had utterly failed to resonate. In fact, as I worked with this feminine image, my attempt to think of her as part of myself gave way to an uncomfortable certainty that instead I was somehow a part of her, not as child to mother, but as witness become the witnessed by something (or someone) far larger than any unresolved object relation or failed relationship through which she might beckon my attention.

In the end, there was simply no gainsaying what had happened. Because my focus on the social sphere had actively repressed the roused presence or "voice" of San Diego, its ignored defensiveness, naturally sheltered, ever on guard, claimed and named after frontier troopers, site of the first military fortifications in California, and dredged and reshaped into the largest and best-armed naval port in the world, had fallen down into and permeated my relationship with my partner and, because I would not listen, had finally blown it apart, the unacknowledged presence of the place thundering into the foreground like cannonfire echoing over an unsuspecting household.

This discovery of the inner power of place opened a passageway into five years of qualitative research up and down El Camino Real, the old Mission Trail connecting San Diego with Sonoma along the coast of Alta, or Upper, California: the reading of histories written about Alta and her various Mission cities and counties; an intensive study of *ecopsychology*, the discipline that deals with our psychological connection to the environment; a foray into *psychohistory*, the analysis of how psychological life shapes historical events; and, finally, the assembly of a new methodology for listening to what I now thought of as the resonant "voice" or trauma of place. My primary question was: if I put aside the anti-terrestrial biases of my culture and regarded coastal California as a psychically active being, viewing her with eyes and ears sensitized by therapy training to hunt for recurring motifs, what would present itself to me?

Initial research supported the impression of parallels between shadowy key motifs alive in heavily developed geographical locales and those at work in human psychic life. Themes of San Diegan defendedness, caginess, and paranoia run all the way back to the Mission days, when padres and soldiers packed Indians into adobe conversion centers, fought off attacking warriors protesting this invasion, and guarded the coast from behind the walls of a Rome-style fort. Klan activity, the aggressive conservatism of city founder Alonzo Horton, the Naval presence and hardware, the Air Force over North Island, Marines in desert training near Oceanside, the police and patrols along the international border, the barricade itself: these are not simple, solid facts of politics or geography, but long-standing expressions of defense and attack, splitting and control. And so it is wherever people live among places that act like magnets, attracting mythologies, pathologies, stories, and lore. *Features of the landscape cross through the frontiers of consciousness to image themselves as psychic beings, but without relinquishing their environmental qualities.* In this they behave something like what psychoanalysis knows as selfobjects: subjects of our experience that feel like aspects of ourselves. *Repress the manifestations of this lively interactivity and they return with symptomatic force, over and over, until they receive a place in a more extended, more ecological, sense of self.*

A careful examination of California's twenty-one Mission towns and all fourteen of her Mission counties uncovered repeating themes and images and echoes roaring and bleeding like feverish, unhealed syndromes shared by people and places alike. In Los Angeles, for example, with its frankly Babylonian collisions and mutual contaminations of nature and spirit, prehistoric bones and teeth emerged from the tarry ooze at La Brea at the dawn of the 1900s in the very center of the enormous cross of asphalt spreading over the face of the future metropolis. Given this showy infiltration (one of countless examples) of cruciform urban progress by the chthonic depths of nature, it is no wonder that the horizontal crosspiece was named the Miracle Mile. It is possible to reimagine the most outlandish spiritual cults springing up in the City of Angels as saber-toothed wing beats or well-oiled flights of fancy.

Idealism, mood, aspiration, and economy in hilly, bipolar San Francisco go to historical extremes and always have, swinging up and down like a peninsular manic depression; gold and silver work on divisive Market Street like lithium medication. Drops from the heights into the depths, from suicides at early Carmel and Big Sur to John Denver's tragic Icarian plunge, predominate in Monterey, its Bay, and its underwater canyons, the deepest to be found off the coast of California. In Sonoma, where an American band of invaders charged in and raised their Bear Flag above the outpost plaza, railroad tycoons and grape-growing industrialists have been bear-flagging real estate ever since.

The state as a whole is not immune to such metaphorically suggestive concatenations. It is as though Alta, portrayed as an island on European maps for centuries after explorers knew otherwise, were some wary, sensitive organism determined to shield itself from human invasion. Adobes and bell towers have dissolved over and over in sudden storms, or fallen to pieces in relentless earthquakes. (The shaker that greeted conquistadors entering Orange County rumbled "for about the length of an Ave Maria.") Spanish sailors up "The Crotch" in the Gulf lost ships to sudden maelstroms; up and down California, more than thirty submerged galleons collect barnacles near the sea cliffs they strove to mount.

A few more examples from a growing list of how what happens in, or to, a given geographical location can become thematic for those nearby:

- A woman working in a conflict-ridden institution whose employees stage a baffling attempt to push a popular leader downhill realizes that she and her coworkers unknowingly repeat a 150-year-old drama whose charismatic key player was likewise unseated. Underlining the persistence of this highly localized echo, the institution bears the name of that earlier leader and sits on property once owned by him.

- A graduate student researching the designs of petroglyphs scattered around a present-day bombing range discovers carved images shaped like bombs, jets, and explosions—images carved hundreds of years before the invention of missiles or aircraft. Indigenous locals attributed these images to the presence of the Thunderbird deity known for centuries to fly over the area.

- Another student preparing to visit a county he has never been to dreams about it the night before his trip. The word "contaminated" occurs throughout the dream. When he arrives at the place, he finds this motif everywhere, from polluted bays and streams to invading species and underground oil spills.

- In a small sample of interviewees asked to describe their experience of a sacred or meaningful place, all describe it as though it were a soothing, healing mentor or spiritual presence.

- A dreamer awakens in a sweat from images of towers of burning flame. A week later he sees them again on television as the largest brushfire in the history of his homeland consumes an area the size of Rhode Island.

- Shortly before a tsunami strikes, five tribes move inland to avoid a flood that destroys their villages. One medicine leader claims that the god responsible for the deluge warned him in a dream.

What qualities distinguish these uncanny connections between dwellers and the land? They are deeply symbolic. They are local. They persist through time, even over many human lifespans. They are registered internally. They tend to organize themselves into discernible syndromes. They resist reduction to either human interiors or environmental externals. And they are often spectacularly interactive, even to the point of showing up as human styles of perception and modes of discourse. In short, what C. G. Jung wrote about the unconscious seems true of the presence of place: *it turns toward us the face that we turn toward it*. Psychologically, shouting down the inner critic who fills fearful minds with doubts and self-loathing only strengthens it; repressing sexuality guarantees its later return in bizarre actings out; reducing spiritual yearnings to the status of childhood longings enlarges them unconsciously into creeds, oughts, and isms. Cover a place's history and vitality in asphalt, concrete, or forgetfulness, and it returns an episode at a time in symptoms, in dreams, in folklore, crime, public politics, or private fights until brought fully into the present through conscious reflection.

A premise to explore, then: *When people inhabit a particular place, its features inhabit their psychological field, in effect becoming extended facets of their selfhood. The more they repress this local, multifaceted sense of environmental presence, the likelier its features will reappear unconsciously as symbolic, animated forces seething from within and from without.*

As the methods evolved for tracking the pain found in folklore, nightmare, romantic conflict, or historical re-enactment back to the "pain" of place with a view to eventually healing them at the root, the question arose as to what to make of healthier locales, such as holy sites and relatively unspoiled expanses of land. The overall framework clearly wanted widening beyond its initial preoccupation with pathology. A freshly re-engaging perspective on the world was needed, a standpoint wide enough to welcome in the reconnective paradigms of psychology, psychohistory, and ecopsychology, yet flexible enough to try out its assumptions anywhere on our highly reactive planet. It should also make way for a deepened understanding of "place" as a nexus of symbolic animated forces, from the actions of animals and the gestures of storms to the fascinations gleaming forth from everyday objects: gemstone facets, shards of glass, ripples across a pristine pond.

This new framework for viewing "human-humus" interactivity offers a reverent outlook on a sentient cosmos as well as a more formal set of practices for minding matter and tending the matter of mind. Its mythopoetic (or "geopoetic") eye envisions the cosmos as nested spheres of animation from minute quanta to distant quasars: a natural world of emplaced beings beckoning our attention through their deep connections with the human interior. Its name is *terrapsychology*, the study of the presence, or soul, of place.

———————

"Animism! Human projection!"—thus resounds the habitual explaining away of any apparent reactivity we observe in the places we inhabit. If places seem to be alive, goes this self-congratulatory logic, it is only because we anthropomorphically endow them with life as self-certain humanism and literal-minded fundamentalism shake hands over an increasingly desolate globe. We, the supposed peak of creation, rose as living beings from a dead world, turned around, and gave it back its sense of liveliness in a kind of animation-at-one-remove before we became Enlightened. A civilization of intelligent robots might well argue one day that they similarly endowed their mysterious human creators with life.

Touted as objectively self-evident, the convenient belief in a lifeless, soulless Earth carries a heavy religious charge because it requires one. Otherwise, polluting, strip-mining, and warming the globe would feel like violent acts of sacrilege. It is no coincidence that a civilization whose economies depend on such violence regards the planet as a heap of insensible material and perforce misinterprets its faces and voices in dreams, art, folklore, and fantasy as purely human expressions. The real wonder is how we promoted ourselves to the center of all things as bipedal bestowers of truth upon the universe. Imagine the astonishment were astronomers to discover a civilization from a Milky Way backwater, one hardly out of the trees, visualizing itself as the very justification of cosmic being—despite its suicidal unwillingness to refrain from desecrating its own tiny corner of the galaxy.

Behind the rush to label animistic cosmologies "regressive" hides a habit of displacing the spaces of deadness in our mechanistic worldview onto the world rather than locating them in ourselves. The true regression is in objectifying the environment to an ecocidal extent undreamed of in the wildest flights of totemistic imagination.

Centuries of looking at matter and nature—and even people—from the outside (as the quantitative sciences inevitably must, even when focused on psychodynamics) have blurred the crucial distinction between *literalized animism*—explaining meteorology or other natural events as being caused by a spirit or arcane force—and the *inner* experience of these events as responsive, ensouled, and full of significance. The first approach conflicts with the canons of Western science; the second need not. In fact, it could complement them while resurrecting a sense of connection to the world. Inwardly, a molting dream monster named "Babushka" chases a dreamer out of a building; outwardly, the polluted Russian River floods communities out of their homes and towns a month or two after the dream. How we experience this conjunction of inner and outer depends on the mode of consciousness we apply: symbolic and interpretive, or conceptual and externalized. Could not disciplined inquiry finally make room for both? Could it not accept the persistent psychological experience of feeling projected *into* by the surround?

This book opens up the question of whether the uncanny aliveness of the locations we inhabit may well be the rule rather than the exception. It is as though *what the conscious mind is trained to see as nonliving places and things, the unconscious reacts to as animated presences and metaphors.* Borderlines and borderlands, sludgy bays and constricted moods, personal complexes and apartment complexes seem to resonate together as events in the world symbolize aspects of the human self and those aspects in turn point back to the features of the world that evolved our remarkable minds.

Does this sense of psychic animation come from us or from the terrain? Do the nonhuman and even the inorganic possess a rudimentary subjectivity? These inquiries have a long cultural, intellectual, and spiritual history. For now, a few points to consider. First, quantitative research cannot observe a subjective experience directly, even in us; all it sees are firing neurons and complex circuits. No inner homunculus, no ghost in the machine, nothing detectable from the outside. Naturally: subjectivity is an *interiority* of matter, not a measurable secretion of it. The more complex the matter, the richer the expression of its inner nature.

Second, if the working model of the psychological (or "transferential") field as identified by psychoanalysis is widened beyond groups of people to include impactful features of the environment, then parallels between ecological and human wounding and well-being need not be explained by reducing either the one to the other or vice versa. Our method can honor them as interactive, multidimensional, interdependent, and symbolically connective and meaningful. In fact, we can interpret them much as we do the images in dreams, where even the most literal elements display a symbolic character. Instead of a psyche confined to human heads, we behold an ecology of the heart, where verdant landscapes moisten verdant souls. Perhaps we are all "animists" in the unconscious.

To a careful "ear," places can "sound" like animated beings. Why not assume for once that they *do* exhibit qualities of animation in the field that dances between them and us? Why not approach them over the bridges of symbol and dream, which they extend, listening *into* them for images and meanings instead of learning *about* them only from outside? Rather than simply representing pieces of ourselves piled up at some random location, could not a chipped street corner, a leaning tree, a spindly arbor each open a doorway into a fuller sense of belonging, emplacement, and consciousness?

Terrapsychology is the study of how the currents of this aliveness, reactivity, interiority, or psychic animation of a geographical location and its creatures and features interact deeply with our own. It offers descriptions of this interaction, methods for registering it, and practices for managing it. Because we assume a confluence of sensitivities—namely, ours with the places we wish to tend—*qualitative* methods of direct encounter receive more space in this book than *quantitative* strategies, which regard a living presence as an object to be measured or controlled. Our endeavor is not merely to pinpoint matter from an "objective," impersonal distance, but to re-engage it more fully, heart and soul.

Here your investigator is happy to report that such forays into intersubjective animism, or *interanimism*, have not deprived him of his ability to juggle equations, understand new scientific discoveries, or operate the computer on which he types these words. The working assumption that the world is reactively sensitive in ways not measurable but open to demonstration has not packed him off to medievalism or even farther back, nor left him stranded in archaic superstition, nor banished him from the artificially brilliant world of the empirical, never again to enjoy the benefits of medicine, automation, or the Periodic Table.

To an ear tuned to place, the fear of regressing into hopeless "primitivism" and the fear of falling off a flat world's edge grate like the same dreary chant played in different keys. It is long past time to change our tune. A perspective worthy of its subjects (not objects) of inquiry would require the sophistication to "put away childish things" and leave the clacking billiard balls of causality and reductionism on the table where they belong. We have played enough dangerous games with matter. Our willingness to risk it reflects an institutionalized failure to connect two great traditions of knowledge: the empirically scientific and the richly animistic. What after all is relentless reductionism but a defense against the numinous power of the world's animation?

A primary goal of terrapsychology is to find out more about the depths of relations between people and places, the human soul and the soul of locale (*genius loci*). By doing so, it strives to play a meaningful part in ending the war against nature that is poisoning the ecosphere while mutating lethally into suicidal antiworlds such as isms and ideologies, spreading states of exile and warfare, and displacing what remains of collective human sanity.

Section 1 of this book offers a brief history of our psychological exile from the sense of indigenous rootedness and belonging (Chapter 1), which has resulted not only in the rise of science and industrial civilization, but in attempts to reconnect self and world by developing psychology and ecopsychology (Chapter 2). Section 2 introduces Terrapsychological Inquiry, that is, the specific research methodology of terrapsychology (Chapters 3-5). Section 3 delineates four specific areas of inquiry: *archetypal geography* (Chapter 6), the study of how certain mythological figures seem to dwell in specific landscapes (Prometheus, for example, seems to favor Switzerland, that home of so many reformers and innovators, including C. G. Jung); *dialogical alchemy* (Chapter 7), the ancient, pre-industrial, and now terrapsychological exploration of matter's apparently subjective qualities; and *lorecasting* (Chapter 8), an attempt to re-imagine natural disasters, meteorological events, and sacred sites as expressions of Terra's inward, symbolic "speech."

It is impossible to ignore the context of global deterioration in which this new perspective of terrapsychology makes its appearance. With pandemics, ecological destruction, and the largest mass extinctions ever, accelerating on every side, leaders of the "free" world play at politics as though business as usual were still compatible with survival—human survival or anything else's. Ordinary environmentalism having proved ineffectual in halting what William Blake described as "the dark satanic mills" converting our world into a literal underworld, a case must now be made for indigenous ecological values carried into an interanimistic concern for places as presences impacting our survival and psychological well-being just as ours impact what remains of their integrity. Only that level of urgency has given me the boldness to publish such exploratory work. (A scribble on my desk suggests: "Act as though the empire had already fallen.")

My hope is that this new terrapsychological primer will encourage "world therapists" to explore how the cracks in stones and the veins of leaves parallel the lineaments of the human soul.

Terra Nova: Earthly Leave-Takings as Preludes to Re-engagement

However much we pride ourselves on those magnificent things human beings have done and made, the final criterion by which all human creations will be judged is the extent that they are consonant with the natural world, of which humans are a part.

—Paul Shepard

CHAPTER ONE

The Flaming Sword: A Brief History of the Ideological Empire over Matter

And the Lord God said, Behold, the man is become as one of us, to know good and evil: and now, lest he put forth his hand, and take also of the tree of life, and eat, and live for ever:

Therefore the Lord God sent him forth from the garden of Eden, to till the ground from whence he was taken.

So he drove out the man; and he placed at the east of the garden of Eden Cherubims, and a flaming sword which turned every way, to keep the way of the tree of life.

—Genesis 3:22-24

From long before the coming of the conquering Cross and Sword, in the days when the gods and their lands had not been separated, it was common knowledge that if the bonds holding together a people with their place, their ancestors, and their divinities were broken, their souls would sicken and their society would fall. This perspective would have recognized unnatural catastrophes such as organized warfare, institutionalized racism and sexism, the will to dominate, planet-wasting consumerism, greed, disease, poverty, pollution, and global warming as unravelings in the weave of an ancient fabric of irreplaceable preciousness.

In our day, however, when the feel for intricate ties between self and surround has been lost, the resulting disasters are explained away as "human nature." We bomb and waste, attack and spend, desertify the land and darken the sky because "that's just how we are"—as though these problems have always been with us. But have they?

The best evidence to date indicates that organized, systematized warfare marked by ordered movements of armed troops goes back roughly only 10,000 years.[1] Organized religion is also only a few millennia old, running back to the Aryans in India, to the time of the Hebrew Prophets, and to Zoroaster of Persia's Manichean division of the universe into Good and Evil. Widespread pollution, industrial waste, chronic hunger, and unchecked economic opportunism were all similarly nonexistent until fairly recently in history. Rampant disease did not threaten the world's populations until livestock was domesticated—goats and sheep first, other animals later—following the long Agricultural Revolution.

Understanding the sundering of our inner ties to the living land requires a very brief look at how our world-girdling empire over matter first came into being, and with it the loss of our sense of Earth as sacred.

Leaving the Garden: The Long Flight out of the Fertile Crescent

Something quite new happened at the end of a million years of human history and prehistory: rows of crops were planted in the Fertile Crescent of the Middle East, where farmers grew barley for bread and beer to trade near the Tigris and Euphrates Rivers.[2] After 70,000 frosty years, the last Ice Age was in full retreat, with many of the largest mammals—the mastodon, the giant sloth, the saber-toothed cat, the horned bison, and the highly valued gazelle—extinct as a warming trend and drought swept over the Earth. As hunters turned their attention to other game and the Sun's glare intensified, someone had the idea of growing the same kind of plant in the same row in the same plot of soil. Potentially, this new arrangement could feed many more people than hunting or gathering, an especially useful accomplishment given the heightened need to remain near reliable sources of water. With the unexpected warmth encouraging the growth of wild cereals, storing them also made sense.

It would be difficult to overestimate just how propitious a place the Fertile Crescent had become for this kind of novel human labor. Among its unusually high diversity of plants grew 32 of the world's 56 prize grasses and six of the contemporary world's twelve biggest crops. The climate favored not only rare cereals (six of the world's eight most important) and self-pollinating plants, but fast-growing annuals that produced large seeds. High-energy cereals could be collected and stored there, a fact that led to technologies such as sickles, baskets, mortar-grinding, grain-roasting, and other useful food production methods, which peaked around 8500 B.C.E. Whatever hunter-gatherers still remained were vastly outnumbered by rising settled populations (one acre feeds 10 to 100 times more farmers than gatherers), their hunting skills less and less valuable as game declined.[3]

Other animals were proving increasingly useful: they provided milk, meat, fertilizer, transport, wool, leather, and the plowing power needed to lay open tougher soils. Four of the five most important domesticatable animals lived locally, there at a future crossroads and on a key east-west trade route: cow, goat, sheep, and pig. The resulting progression is not difficult to visualize: a band of people settling near fields that they depend on for trade and food; women tilling and planting; workers weeding the fields; builders erecting fences to protect the crops; accountants figuring out what to barter; warriors organizing to fend off marauders; and then: small villages to house these laboring groups of people; sturdy walls to ring the villages; temples to house collective relics; and so onward and upward as the first urban centers of antiquity spread, their massing populations increasingly dependent on slavery, animal domestication, and the spoils of war. Food surpluses allowed specialists to work on ever more sophisticated tools and technics, particularly writing, wheels, and weapons of war. The natural horizontal lay of the continent helped them expand ever outward.[4]

Although the horse would not be domesticated until 4000 B.C.E., allowing warriors from the steppes north of the Black Sea to sweep down into Old Europe, replace its indigenous languages with Indo-European, subjugate its feminine authorities, and suppress its goddesses, the ancient Western bifurcation between wild and tame, outside and in, gatherers and growers, and nature and mind had begun.

The Sword's Other Edge: The Rise of Antisocial Antiworlds

Some would argue that the progression just detailed constituted a colossal collective mistake; that humanity was wrong to plow, wrong to plant, wrong to leave the garden. Certainly it opened enough social and psychological space to consider the natural world as a separate Other, subject to potential manipulation and control. Re-imagining the entire movement up and out as a foundational but largely unconscious differentiation or evolution, an idea to be taken up again in Chapter 8, allows for the possibility of its being neither gloriously progressive nor heinously ill-fated,[5] but a collective development susceptible to a dangerous one-sidedness.

For all they can store, produce, and tabulate, post-horticultural civilizations carry an in-built weakness, like a highly trained muscle group faced with a strain not prepared for. Their growing dependency on specialization multiplies opportunities for ambitious individuals (of the type who really do not feel at home in the world) to seize control of all that thickening, rising, and expanding centralization of planning, productivity, fecundity, and power, and to become the most feared and tyrannical of leaders.

> After the rise of the Fertile Crescent states in the fourth millennium B.C., the center of power initially remained in the Fertile Crescent, rotating between empires such as those of Babylon, the Hittites, Assyria, and Persia. With the Greek conquest of all advanced societies from Greece east to India under Alexander the Great in the late fourth century B.C., power finally made its first shift irrevocably westward. It shifted farther west with Rome's conquest of Greece in the second century B.C., and after the fall of the Roman Empire it eventually moved again, to western and northern Europe.[6]

The levers through which the ambitious could obtain control were right at hand. Master accountancy records. Priestly hierarchies to encourage the crops. Educational texts. People organized into specialties such as cook, farmer, warrior, figurer, blesser, dung-shoveler. Who will organize these groups is the first question of post-horticultural organization, and the second is even more important: Who would want such a job? To attempt an answer requires a psychohistorical extrapolation.

The controlling perfectionists of the species wanted the job, those sons of Saturn who bask in procedure and revel in power over others. And like Saturn, the Roman god of agriculture and order imposed from above, and like their incorporated counterparts today, they wanted very badly to systematize their power. The world was not enough for them because it demanded the very qualities that many of them lacked: cooperativeness, wisdom, openness, imagination, courage of heart, face-to-face problem-solving, communal conflict reconciliation—what the sports-obsessed of our day call "teamwork."

Antisocial solitaries filled with fear and chronic paranoia do not dialog or negotiate well and, ever on the lookout for some Jupiter out to overthrow them, they don't like teamwork either. To compensate for their insufficiencies, to shore up their sense of importance, the most aggressive among them seek to *own* the team instead, while shouldering aside less heavy-handed rulers perceived as dangerous rivals for power. As non-cooperators (formerly weeded out by the requirements of survival) assumed control, leaders who ruled with a wiser or gentler style were forced to defend themselves more and more frequently against a variety of vicious but psychologically immature attacks: deceptive propaganda, character assassination, military conquest, outright murder. One can see this development at work today.[7]

Yet, as with most new developments, this increasing degree of specialization showed the world a bright side as well as a shadow. It proved efficient, of course, in assigning tasks and keeping track of what was grown and made where. It set aside resources, time, and opportunity for the perfection of skills exercised by talented individuals. It shielded at least some of the injured, sick, and disabled from the brute, lethal fact of evolutionary selection pressures. To the lasting pain of people and planet, however, it also shielded the occasional pathological seeker of power from the consequences of his actions.

Working now by force and now by persuasion, but always by power-driven expediency, the paranoically ambitious who hated and feared the tangible world pushed, manipulated, deceived, and intimidated until they ran the priesthood, the guild, the farming cooperative, the warrior caste, and when even that did not silence the evil demon of restless unbelonging, they plotted to own, not just one team, or ten, but all of them. To what end? Greater human comfort? Peace on Earth? No: *the establishment of an artificial, centralized world—an antiworld—where they could finally feel at home and in control* behind closed doors, closed fences, and closed gates. As Milton's Satan summed it up for all such pitiable people, it is better to reign in hell than serve in heaven.

Under self-consolidating ruling elites, centralized power, humanity's oldest protection racket, reinforced the concentration of people around croplands and temples, the new idealization of fertility, the subsequent confinement and devaluation of women, and the believers, enforcers, propagandists, and workers produced by the consecrated soaring birthrates endemic to settled living.

It was not that these early foreshadowings of metropolis and empire grew unsustainable over time. They never were to begin with. Margined off, fertilized, and irrigated into forced overabundance, the land around these parasitic urban concentrations eventually wore down until exhaustion outside the walls echoed the violence organized within them. It is no accident that sedentary Sumer, situated within the Fertile Crescent, near fabled Eden, claims the dubious double distinction of becoming not only the world's first state (shortly before pharaonic Egypt) but also the first state to become unsustainable, once the saltine soils of formerly arable fields began to crack and erode and exiled farming communities spread their consumptive habits west and east across Europe.

> The Sumerians gave way to the Akkadians, from the surrounding desert, who in turn were squelched by the First Babylonian Empire in around 1900 BC, who were conquered by the Chaldeans, thus initiating the Second Babylonian Empire in 612 BC, which gave way to the Persian invasion in 539 BC. Interspersed were Hittites and Hurrians and other interlopers.[8]

Meanwhile, the felt bifurcation of self and world hardened into doctrine.

CARVING OUT THE SPLIT: I THINK, THEREFORE I FENCE

The ascension of the Antiworld was a slow one, unfolding over many centuries, and it did not take place unopposed. Historically key figures such as Socrates, Isaiah, Zoroaster, the Buddha, Lao Tse, Kung Fu-Tse (Confucius), Jesus, and the Prophet Muhammad bravely countered the realpolitikal agendas of the empire-builders by insisting on the primacy of ethical behavior. "Humaneness is more important than fire and water." "God's radiance fills the heavens and the earth." "The Kingdom is in your midst." Yet whatever they taught about well-grounded faith, and however rooted their teachings in native soil, they were quickly re-interpreted by literal-minded followers who, donning robes, crowns, and scepters, translated their subtle parables and organic metaphors into systems and dogmas and other rigidified abstractions—"teaching as doctrines the precepts of men," as Jesus had seen in his day. There seems to be a law in human affairs that an emphasis on another world increases in step with an accumulation of power in this one.

As Augustine (354-430 B.C.E) contemplated the fall of the Roman Empire (caused in part by the flooding of silver mines in Spain when digging struck down to the water table) and the need for a sense of community and belonging, the Church found vindication for its emphasis on the hereafter in Plato's work, once it was re-interpreted as a classical exposition of otherworldly philosophizing. Did not the great thinker himself believe in eternal Forms, heavenly prototypes or archetypes, which only the noblest intellects could effectively catch sight of? Was humanity's true home therefore not on earth, but in an imperishable Beyond? And Aristotle, a fifth-century contemporary of Plato's, rediscovered by the West via Islamic and Byzantine sources: true, he was a naturalist, but did not his emphasis on Reason and his categories of comprehension prepare the way for the intellectual appreciation of the ruling God behind the world, the rational God of Thomas Aquinas and the Scholastics who came after him?

Arguments about the number of angels that could stand on a pin's head might seem silly now, but they gave birth to conceptual systems of a complexity never seen before as a heightened sense of individuality came forth from a new emphasis on personal salvation.

The accelerating split between subject and object, inner and outer, and self and world did not confine itself to religious circles of influence. Following Augustine, René Descartes—philosopher, mathematician, orphan, Christian, and inventor of the coordinate system of points and gridded crosses—advised the philosopher to begin his work by first doubting everything but doubt itself, as though an evil demon were quietly whispering uncertainties into one's ear. Descartes posited that (1) human thought is the one undeniable reality; (2) what we think gives shape to our sense of existence; (3) thought is separate from the world of matter outside the mind; and (4) mind is separate from the world of nature. These four blows proved lethal, philosophically speaking, to the connective tissue binding the mortal self to the ageless globe around it. Many gentlemen of his time wore a sword, but Descartes wielded concepts of far sharper cutting power than his dueling blade.

Of course, disease, warfare, and the other institutionally entrenched symptoms mentioned above were well along in their development before he and his very straight edge came around, but his sweeping cuts carved out the ancient theme fermenting beneath them all into its starkest definition yet: *the unnatural but religiously, economically, and politically expedient distancing of self from its psychological emplacement in the world.*

Into that gap rushed the thickening hard science of Copernicus, Bacon, Kepler, Galileo, Newton—but, behind and even within this development, there was also a renewed sense of earthly presence.

"O Earth, O Earth, Return!"

The reappearance of heavily repressed naturalistic images of earthly beauty (denied the full experiential authentication they had once received) was only a matter of time. In the fifteenth century, as negative numbers first surfaced in the West ("integer" from the Latin for "untouched") and Greek stories spread about a dark planetary twin, an Antichthon ("Counterearth") circling the Sun's far side, the Age of Exploration set out in search of strangely compelling visions of heaven on Earth: the Northwest Passage, Cities of Cibola, Straits of Anion, El Dorado, Shangri-La, the Grand Quivira, the Fountain of Youth. But the greed which literalized these welcoming images of terrestrial renewal into golden palaces and fabulous seaways placed them out of reach. Mad Columbus claimed to have found not only India and the Orient, but the Terrestrial Paradise itself just before confiding to the Spanish court his disoriented belief about the actual shape of the Earth. It was not round after all, he wrote, but mounded like a woman's breast.[9]

The milk and honey of silver and gold bullion forcibly sucked from the paradisal New World founded the first stock market, in Antwerp, and, flooding at length into European banks, fed the machineries of the Industrial Revolution as the victims of conquest died by the millions at the source.

A long line of thinkers, including John Locke, Immanuel Kant, and David Hume, had continued the Cartesian project of relegating aliveness and presence solely to the inner world as the feeling for place gave way to the concept of space.[10] Kant in particular insisted that outer reality is not only unanimated, but ultimately unknowable, its apparent principles of organization—time, space, causality—actually bestowed by the mind. But with Darwin, Rousseau, Nietzsche, Schelling, and Schopenhauer, new influxes of Far Eastern literature and thought, and Romantic painting and music, this idea began to reverse itself. Categories of thought might arise from within, but basic principles of organization ultimately derived from nature itself. In Blake, Hawthorne, Melville, van Gogh, Monet, Shelley, Goethe, and Beethoven, Nietzsche's battle cry from *Thus Spake Zarathustra* was receiving its due: Break the maxims of those who slander the world. Frameworks of scientific, religious, and philosophical thought were looking much more like metaphors (or "meta-narratives," as Lyotard would argue) through which shone the light of the natural world, a world which C. G. Jung, among others, said held soul.

As events accelerated, fewer and fewer were fooled by modernity's progressive face. If the liberatory and civil rights movements budding forth everywhere shared one commonality, it was an embodied refusal to be taken in by all the promissory chatter about technological redemption and new world orders while people and places went under the wheels of progress. Luddites and socialists jammed wrenches into the cogs. Thoreau, Gandhi, and Martin Luther King, Jr. enriched the discourse of resistance by forging the instruments of nonviolent protest. Rosa Parks refused to sit down, Gloria Steinem refused to serve drinks, and Aung San Suu Kyi refused to be silent when armed bullies tried to beat Burma into Myanmar. Writing about revolt, Camus said one could reject all of history but keep the sea and the stars.[11]

On the ecological side of the house, concern with the environment was nothing new. Native Americans had managed a continent ecologically for millennia. The first known wildlife protection law was passed during the reign of Ashoka of India (256 B.C.E.). The shogun Tokagawa ordered tree seedlings planted. But in the 1700s, environmentalism began to simmer like steam from the roots of nature-loving Romanticism. To the surprise of many caught in dreams of progress, poets began writing about the devastation wreaked by unbridled colonialism. They were perhaps the first non-native people to feel the link between the flesh of the world and the state of their souls. In England, William Blake had given a voice to orphans left out in the cold of streets turned black by factory smoke, and human and ecological health and illness became harder and harder to think of as separate. Thoreau published his book *Walden* in 1854, fourteen years before John Muir moved to his beloved Yosemite, the park he would protect. Their efforts combined with Aldo Leopold's *Sand County Almanac* (1948), which called for extending the idea of ethics to the land, Rachel Carson's *Silent Spring* (1962), which described the dangers of pesticides and industrial pollution, and Barry Commoner's *The Closing Circle* (1971), which showed technology as problem rather than solution, and the result was modern environmentalism as a coherent force in public affairs. Native Americans' calls for social justice and environmental sanity grew stronger and more insistent as elaborate ideologies of social domination continued to deconstruct themselves, with help from existentialism and postmodernism:

> The rise of fascism, two world wars, de-colonisation, seismic technological change, environmental and ecological disaster, the information explosion, the growth of exploitative and non-accountable global capitalism, with its commodification of labour in the 'developed' West and the worsening dispossession of the toiling masses across the underdeveloped globe, have all but destroyed the meta-narratives that legitimized both science and history as foundations of what has been regarded as an inexorable trend towards individual freedom and the self-conscious improvement of the human condition.[12]

Nevertheless, a key justification of the industrial-military juggernaut's violent course has never been successfully challenged. With economies now dependent upon belief in Earth's material inexhaustibility, a bountiful Columbian breast that would never run dry, the fear of nature as evil and fallen has congealed into this world-deserting era's most fervent prejudice, superstition, and excuse: that matter is dead and buried—and therefore available for unchecked plundering—as the numbers representing mass extinction, mass pollution, mass hunger and thirst, unregulated weapons of mass consumption, and the other perennial ills mentioned above rise skyward out of sight and sense faster than the flight of a sword-bearing cherub.

Houston, we have a problem.

> These dominant mythologies of thinking—an anthropocentric world, a secularized promised land, unlimited progress, a triumphalist futurity of complete domination over the natural order and our natural instincts—prevent us from facing suffering. They require denial, disavowal, repression, and psychic numbing to keep their belief systems intact. The consequence to us is the inability to experience the actual suffering these narratives result in: the suffering of earth, the suffering of place, the suffering of our human and nonhuman communities, and our own suffering.[13]

As this observation by Laura Mitchell suggests, the time has come to realize without further illusions that ecocide and its attendant ills, from fortified outposts to fortified cereals, are too high a price to pay any longer for the dangerous fantasy of omnipotent actors and sons of Saturn occupying the stage of a dead world.

Every indigenous culture without exception has insisted that the soulful Earth and its creatures address us continually with unceasing reminders of our responsibilities as thinking animals in the scheme of things. It is time to take this claim seriously.

> Isn't the return to Eden, the Homecoming, to find that, after all, we never left the Garden and all the earth is sacred?[14]

If implacably longstanding growths such as warfare and poverty, waste and greed are too entangled to cut back from their present complexity, the option remains of deconstructing the person-place alienation that props them up. This is where psychology and ecopsychology come in, both arising in step with worldwide movements of political and environmental liberation fanning out over a troubled globe. Watching this change of focus expand outward will prepare us for one of the most important questions there can be, and one that planetwide survival may well hinge upon today:

If the wounded Earth is indeed calling out to us, what must we do to hear it?

There appears to be a law that when creatures have reached the level of consciousness, as men have, they must become conscious of the creation; they must learn how they fit into it and what its needs are and what it requires of them, or else pay a terrible penalty: the spirit of the creation will go out of them, and they will become destructive; the very earth will depart from them and go where they cannot follow.

—Wendell Berry

CHAPTER TWO

Widening Rejoinings: From Psychology to Ecopsychology and Beyond

Because we live in the hardedged season,
where plastic brittle and gleaming shines
and in this space that is cornered and angled,
we do not notice wet, moist, the significant
drops falling in perfect spheres
that are the certain measures of our minds ....

—Paula Gunn Allen, "Kopis'taya
(A Gathering of Spirits)"

For most of the human past, the presence of place *was* our unconscious. What we now regard as mood swings, sudden lows, and inexplicable complexes roved the hills and vales wearing the faces of brooding spirits. Psychology appeared as this long tradition went under the wheels of progress. The first psychological laboratories opened in 1875: four slim years after anthropologist Edward Taylor marveled that the "primitives" he was studying believed that the world was ensouled. The sprites and spirits had now moved inside; the wizards donned lab coats; and the trolls, we thought, could be medicated.

Although *psychology* ("study of soul") extends at least as far back as 1851,[1] psychology of the deep sort, which gave an ear to unvoiced experiences exiled to the margins of culture and consciousness, did not appear until 1885, when Pierre Janet published a paper on his patient "Leonie."[2] Trained in philosophy and medicine, Janet worked in the hospital in Le Havre, France on an approach to treatment ("psychological analysis") that interpreted symptoms as dissociative expressions of "subconscious" trauma and that sought to manage the *"rapport magnetique"* (transference), the patient's emotional focus on the doctor. In Vienna, Sigmund Freud and Josef Breuer collaborated on *Studies in Hysteria* (1895), a book about using emotional catharsis in treatment. By 1900 C. G. Jung was seeing psychotic patients at the Burgholzli mental hospital in Switzerland; from there his researches linking delayed reactions to stimulus words with psychological conflict caught Freud's attention and inaugurated Jung's international reputation. "Depth psychology," psychiatrist Eugen Bleuler named the field from which sprang the subsequent client-therapist treatment modalities employed by Janet, Freud, and Jung to heal self-alienation by restoring the dialog between conscious and unconscious mental life.

Although this growing body of multidisciplinary work made the biological face of nature—instinct, affect, the body—its abiding concern, it also harbored an unhelpful and rather solipsistic introversion. Janet tried to replace painful memories with pleasant ones without honoring the original trauma, only to find his own work similarly pushed into the background. Freud's and Karl Abraham's insistence that instinctual passions take precedence over outer events displayed a shocking disregard for the realities of sexual abuse and post-traumatic combat stress; the destructive habit of reducing psychic distress or social injustice to the pathology of the sufferer (e.g., "You have a problem with that person because he or she reminds you of something in you") persists to this day. Alfred Adler, another founding depth psychologist, was among the first to question this overemphasis on an inner world divorced from the outer by showing how dreams, symptoms, and other expressions of "the unconscious" achieved real goals in the patient's outer world.[3]

Even so, no one asked as yet whether the "hysteria" (fainting spells, numbness, dissociation, and paralysis) they were trying to treat might be saying something not only about the widespread oppression of the women who suffered from it, but about the fainting biosphere under siege by Victorian technology. Nightmares and neuroses remained conceptually split off from the world from which they sprang and with which they resonated. For even the boldest thinkers, brought up as they were on the doorstep of the Enlightenment, the nature to which they sought to reconnect consciousness remained the human one. As we will see in Chapter 6, however, C. G. Jung proved a noteworthy exception to the cultural habit of ascribing mindfulness to man and deadness to the natural world. As his thought progressed and deepened, he became more and more convinced that qualities of psyche and spirit inhabit the nonhuman world.[4] His polycentric emphasis on a psyche with multiple centers of mutual interaction came close indeed to re-visioning the personality as a kind of imaginal ecosystem.

ECOPSYCHOLOGICAL FOREBEARS

As psychology continued to differentiate, with some perspectives emphasizing clinical findings, others adhering to empirically based research, and most ignoring the possibility of deep inner bonds with the environment, more and more people grew aware that all was not well ecologically with Earth and therefore all not well with her increasingly urbanized inhabitants.

Smog had been a problem in Imperial Rome, whose citizens called it "heavy air." As long ago as 1938, British engineer George Callendar had compiled evidence from two hundred weather stations to conclude that global atmospheric temperature was rising. By 1949, when the United Nations held the first international environmental conference, and future activist Gary Snyder began working for the U.S. Forest Service, killer fogs in London, lead in U.S. gasoline, fish and whales gone from the oceans, and vanishing forests everywhere were receiving widespread attention, not only from the public, but from ecological investigators unlocking connections that psychologists and environmentalists had missed while working away separately.

Penetrating questions had been piling up for decades like silver keys by the fistful. Soon to be joined by scholars Bill Devall, George Sessions, and Dolores LaChapelle, Norwegian thinker Arne Naess asked whether we needed to promote a shallow stewardship that peddles "wise use" Band-Aids, or instead practice a "deep ecology" (1973), one that calls into question the destructive cultural assumptions that fuel the human-centered sense of global entitlement. How and why did so many stop seeing themselves as fellow members of a planetary ecocommunity? What is gained and what is lost by regarding human beings as nature's masters? Deep ecologists countered this egocentric habit of thought with a platform geared toward identification with the natural world and transcendence of anthropocentrism.[5]

Feminists replied that as worthy as such a platform sounds, it fails to hold civilization's traditional male power structure to account. Men socialized in cultures that disempower women tend to equate femininity with "Mother" Nature, to the detriment of both. The traditionalist argument that women are closer to nature because they can give birth defines women solely in terms of their reproductive capacity and the natural world in terms of its supposed femininity. The obvious implication is that both are mere objects in need of taming and control. In 1974, the year ecological activist Peter Berg and conservationist Raymond Dasmann coined the term "bioregion" to describe an ecologically (and culturally) distinct geography to emphasize the localized sense of place, Françoise d'Eaubonne's *La Féminisme ou la Mort* introduced the term *ecofeminism* ("écoféminisme"), and with it a flurry of explorations into similarities between how men exploit the natural world and how they exploit women, with both manipulations operating as a denial of the fact of interdependency. Feminist scholar Susan Griffin examined the history of this cultural trend toward manipulation and dual objectification in her 1978 book *Woman and Nature: The Roaring Inside Her.*

The year 1978 was itself a kind of watershed. As Lois Gibbs investigated the toxic Love Canal in New York, biologist David Ehrenfeld diagnosed the belief that humans can solve, know, and do anything as an historically conditioned state of inflation, naturalist John A. Livingston attacked human arrogance and technological self-domestication, and Robert Bullard wrote his "Cancer Alley" report on DDT water pollution in Alabama. In the same year, farmer-scholar Wendell Berry published *The Unsettling of America*, its essays drawing sharp correlations between perceived uprootedness, alienation from the body, irresponsibility toward the land, and our lack of caring for each other. As though in response, "geologian" Thomas Berry published his "New Story" of a "cosmogenesis" still evolving—and evolving us along with it. He maintained high hopes that humans would embrace a view of the universe as an integrated whole to which they too belong.[6]

A year later (1979), James Lovelock published thoughts on the Gaia Hypothesis, developed by him and biologist Lynn Margulis to rethink Earth as a single self-balancing system. The following year anthropologist Dian Fossey wrote *Gorillas in the Mist*. Jane Goodall's work with chimpanzees in Africa made their kinship with us apparent to millions who read her articles in *National Geographic*.

In the political sphere, the idea of bioregions had evolved into *bioregionalism*, with its call to re-inhabit the lands where we live, study their ecologies and history, get to know their plant and animal life, and take responsibility for keeping their resources and human needs in balance.[7] This renewed emphasis on getting local, with political demarcations readjusted to match the contours of the land, found an echo in the social sphere. Can a true democracy stretch over millions of square miles, and serve millions of people who never meet face to face? Can one politician adequately represent hundreds or thousands? Writer and environmental restorer Jim Dodge's conclusion: absurd. Modern democracy did not grow up inside the confines of empire, but in reaction against them, one politically active township at a time. If something is wrong, philosopher and economist Leopold Kohr added, then something is too big.[8]

If anything, the shameless environmental disregard foreshadowed by George H. W. Bush's 1981 proposal to end the phase-out of leaded gasoline (repeatedly shown to be toxic), a disregard that had been exemplified time and again throughout the blissfully disembodied Reagan Administration, only increased the urgency of the questions being posed about the resonances between ecological damage and human well-being. If you cage a species such as ours in a world of artifacts in which it was never designed to dwell, what happens? A *techno-addiction* that anesthetizes the "original wound" of shock and emptiness, observed Chellis Glendinning, while only making them worse.[9] Greed, cites physicist and activist Vandana Shiva, coiner of the label "maldevelopment," from her knowledge of the shadow of industry in India.[10] Intense psychic isolation, adds activist writer Jerry Mander, as we forget that by ringing ourselves in surfaces and circuits, we live shut away inside our own externalized minds.[11] Buddhist and systems theorist Joanna Macy's haunting term for this destructive loop of alienation is *environmental despair*.[20] To work with it, Macy and philosopher John Seed designed a Council of All Beings to breach the denial that numbs us to the pain of the natural world, foster revisualization of our rootedness in that world, and promote "thinking like a mountain" and rituals of reconnection to land, plants, and animals. Professors Allen Kanner and Mary Gomes directed an "Altars of Extinction" project at Sonoma State to mourn the animal and insect life that will never return. For environmental education professor David Orr, teaching "ecological literacy"[13] could take another constructive step toward remembering our place in a world under daily attack by the inadequately restrained capitalism also critiqued by socialist anarchist Murray Bookchin, for whom classism and hierarchy serve as paradigms for the domination of nature.

Education or re-education of one kind or another had shown itself key to the efficacy of every school of both psychotherapy and its ecological counterparts. So it would prove to ecopsychology as two great traditions—psychology and environmentalism—finally joined hands.

BRIDGING MIND AND EARTH: ECOPSYCHOLOGY

Psychologist Robert Greenway had been talking with a group of scholars about "psychoecology" since 1963, when he wrote a short paper to discuss a merging of psychology and ecology.[14] He had watched the slow ecological destruction of Palo Alto and the Silicon Valley, and while a graduate student at Brandeis in Boston he had worked with psychologist Abraham Maslow and attended meetings or lectures with psychologists Erik Erikson, Rollo May, and Carl Rogers and writer Aldous Huxley. With Art Warmouth and other scholars in the "psychoecology" group, Greenway talked about Jung, Piaget's developmental psychology, Karen Horney's brand of psychoanalysis, theories of the philosopher-educator John Dewey, Paul Shepard, John Steinbeck's California, the ego psychologist Heinz Hartmann, the "I-Thou" of Martin Buber, Paul Goodman, who had written about community and urban planning, and Gregory Bateson, who was working on systems theory. By 1968, Greenway had relocated to the Bay Area and was conducting wilderness excursions with his students at Sonoma State.

In 1990, Mary Gomes, an assistant professor of psychology at Holy Names College in Oakland, convened a multidisciplinary study group in Berkeley to discuss what would evolve into ecopsychology. Greenway was one of the participants, as was psychologist Allen Kanner and environmental consultant and educator Elan Shapiro. Environmental science, the deep and transpersonal psychologies, Taoist thought, shamanist traditions, wilderness work, the role of research: it was all on the table, not as an eclectic jumble, but as diagrams of solid bridges rebuilt time and again over centuries of artificial barriers raised to wall out the presence of place. Sciences, beliefs, rituals, and conceptual systems had come and gone; but certain bridges held. How to understand what they were made of? How to open the floodgates below them to spill active forces into the interspecies gradients and channels of planetary restoration?

Social critic, philosopher, and historian Theodore Roszak heard about this group while writing the seminal book *The Voice of the Earth* (1992), which explained the need for what was eventually called "ecopsychology," a bridge spanning the psychological and the ecological, person and place, environment and self, mental health and planetary integrity. A barrier had finally gone down between the healer's ear and a wounded world. Roszak's book began immediately with a critique of modern psychology's habit of removing the self from its environment:

> Once upon a time, all psychologies were "ecopsychologies." Those who sought to heal the soul took it for granted that human nature is densely embedded in the world we share with animal, vegetable, mineral, and all the unseen powers of the cosmos. … It is peculiarly the psychiatry of modern Western society that has split the "inner" life from the "outer" world—as if what was inside of us was not also inside the universe, something real, consequential, and inseparable from our study of the natural world.[15]

Criticism of modern psychology's limiting its scope to the individual's inner workings with minimal regard for the surrounding world also came from within the field of psychology itself. In the same year *The Voice of the Earth* appeared in print, psychologist James Hillman and writer Michael Ventura taped a provocative series of conversations about the impact of psychology on life in and out of the consulting room called *We've Had a Hundred Years of Psychotherapy, and the World's Getting Worse*. They offered the following rebuke, challenging psychology's focus on the consulting room to the disregard of the community:

> Every time we try to deal with our outrage over the freeway, our misery over the office and the lighting and the crappy furniture, the crime on the streets, whatever—every time we try to deal with that by going to therapy with our rage and fear, we're depriving the political world of something. And therapy, in its crazy way, by emphasizing the inner soul and ignoring the outer soul, supports the decline of the actual world. Yet therapy goes on blindly believing that it's curing the outer world by making better people.[16]

Not alone did the psychology industry benefit from this inward turn. Ecopsychologists soon realized that *every* industry, political party, social program, sect, corporation, institution, school, and power bloc afraid of the power of intelligent outrage sighs with relief at the well-intentioned psychotherapist's assurance that conflict is internal and not ecological, economic, or political; that how people live depends on their own personal choices rather than upon their sex or race or their oppressed position; and that psychology's emphasis on the interior helps change the world "one client at a time."[17] How many German analysts interpreted their patients' fears about an upstart named Hitler as resulting from father problems or overstimulated orifices right up until the Reichstag burned to the ground? No amount of therapeutic analysis of this sort could quench that fire—or address what would sustain the analyzed denizens of a world without forests.

To imagine a paradigm of inner healing that could explore the self in its environmental context meant pushing beyond the boundaries of the narcissistic introversion with which Freud had held psychotherapy spellbound, and in some cases going beyond the confines of the therapist's insulated office. Ecopsychology aimed to serve the dual function of criticizing the cultural, social, and historical arrangements that authorize and support injury to self and world while taking us to the root of who we are as humans situated in a more-than-human setting.[18]

Back in San Francisco, a new collection of thoughtful papers, edited by Roszak, Gomes, and Kanner, was published in 1995—*Ecopsychology: Restoring the Earth, Healing the Mind.* This book contains an impressive array of new ideas, fertile thoughts, wilderness encounters, sorrowful reflections on the declining health of the planet, and useful examples for reattaching affective ties to the natural world. In the book's "Environmental Foreword," agricultural economist Lester R. Brown broadly sketched the goal of this new/old field of ecopsychology:

> At its most ambitious, ecopsychology seeks to redefine sanity within an environmental context. It contends that seeking to heal the soul without reference to the ecological system of which we are an integral part is a form of self-destructive blindness. ... In simple terms, we cannot restore our own health, our sense of well-being, unless we restore the health of the planet.[19]

One of the contributors, Elan Shapiro, provided a metaphor at the heart of this nexus of connections: *reciprocity*. Human and ecological health stand or fall together.

Although at first there was no agreed upon definition of ecopsychology among the therapists, activists, ecologists, and wilderness experts engaged in this new field, this definition eventually surfaced:

> Ecopsychology is the effort to understand, heal, and develop the psychological dimensions of the human-nature relationship (psychological, bio-social-spiritual) through connecting and reconnecting with natural processes in the web of life. At its core, ecopsychology suggests that there is a synergistic relation between planetary and personal well being; that the needs of the one are relevant to the other.[20]

This definition gains substance through practice: conducting rituals of mourning for vanishing hillsides, incorporating plants or animals into a counseling session ("ecotherapy"), leading vision quests, tracking a landscape's signature through literature, analyzing nature-based philosophies, unearthing the emotional dynamics behind ecocidal behavior, pointing out the pathologies and dangers in lifestyles of unchecked consumption, correlating data on the disproportion of minority communities exposed to toxic waste.

From its inception, ecopsychology found itself dogged by a tension well known in academia: should ecopsychology be certified or not as a new and distinct discipline? Opinions quickly polarized. Some of the field's original organizers and contributors believed ecopsychology worked best as a multidisciplinary inquiry untainted by institutionalization. To offer classes or training in it was one thing; to mold it into a school, society, or official body quite another. As psychotherapist Andy Fisher points out: "… [P]roposals to institutionalize ecopsychology may wind up further legitimizing the authority of an oppressive, nature-dominating mental health establishment."[21] Certificates in ecopsychology are now available from various schools, but so far the field has not been subjected to the standardization of any central authority. Although this gives it less legitimacy in the eyes of university departments enamored of quantification, reputation, and control, many ecopsychologists question whether the research and certification procedures for which these departments receive funding are really suitable for exploring the human-nature relationship in any depth.

Like psyche itself, ecopsychology remains a polycentric field sponsoring many voices, many crosscurrents, San Francisco-style dips and rises, multidisciplinary enthusiasms facing off against arguments for greater centralization. So long as no single voice predominates, whether rigidly authoritarian or irresponsibly disorderly, the field will bear comparing with the ecosystems it looks to as elegant paradigms of intelligent self-organization.

A particularly urgent task for ecopsychology is to understand and address the impulsivity, recklessness, denial, and spoiled-child irresponsibility increasingly obvious in "First" World behavior toward the environment. In politics it remains disturbingly flagrant. Ecological philosopher Paul Shepard believed that fully adult humanness depends on consistent contact with the nonhuman world;[16] he coined the term *ontogenetic crippling* for the collective but individually expressed psychological immaturity resulting from the loss of Earth-based rites of passage used by primal cultures.[22] As we are cut off from extended exposure to the natural world that evolved us, raised outside extended networks of loving caregivers, and uninitiated into full psychological adulthood by wise elders, our once natural sense of secure attachment to people and place gives way to a pervasive mood of emptiness and exile covered over by a macho exterior, an envious fear of the undomesticated, and an obsession with control. What were a minority of spoiled paranoiacs back in the Fertile Crescent have become the majority members of entire cultures, too distracted and reckless to care about long-term impacts on personal and planetary health. For Gomes and Kanner, this lingering immaturity often surfaces in the angry reactions directed at concerns about the health of the ecosphere. "When environmentalists suggest that humans respect the integrity of uninhabitable or unwelcoming lands, they provoke outrage similar to that expressed by a domineering husband whose wife decides, without his permission, to spend her Friday nights at, say, a women's ritual circle."[23] Bumper sticker appeals to "Love Your Mother," writes Catherine Roach, merely recall the boy too immature to care about his mother's needs or see past the childish illusion of her inexhaustibility.[24]

James Hillman has described the pain of standing on Civil War battlefields feeling the cry of the blood soaked into the soil underfoot. It is wounding, he said, to shed the national habit of innocence long enough to reflect into damage so encompassing—but easy to mail teddy bears to an Empire City stunned by the World Trade Center disaster.[25] Therapeutic practice has not remained above teddybearism. A shadow aspect of the positive psychologies resides in their cheering on the retreat into tree forts of innocence, shielded from hard questions about injurious patterns of consumption and transportation. Useful in small clinical doses for those who need them, growth and development (i.e., little people becoming big people), access to the inner child, "don't worry, be happy," stuffed animals to hug, affirming self-talk on the Little-Train-that-Could model, avoidance of "negative energy that brings me down," and naughty rebellion against strict parents-within through recourse to mud pies and finger painting are hardly images of personhood or citizenship that lend themselves to realistic self-appraisal in the context of tumultuous global affairs. Fortunately, the state of immaturity is reversible.

A related disconnect rears in the rampant splitting between a global focus and a local one, as though they were mutually exclusive. In the well-meaning postcard pictures of Gaia, Earth, Goddess, or World Soul, where are Los Angeles and Chicago, this village, that neighborhood, the shattered factory down the street with broken windows, like rows of sockets without eyes? And what of the reverse error of keeping the eyes fixed on little plots of soil while unthinkable accumulations of corporate wealth destroy entire landscapes? "Love Your Mother"—no, "Think Globally, Act Locally." Surely opportunities await to act locally and raise Cain everywhere, especially when the greatest "resource" of all, an aroused, sentient planet, insists on swinging into the picture. For all we know, Earth harbors its own forms of activism.

By converting discomforts that are resistant to therapy or medication into conscious distress to be honored and worked through, grounded, reflective ecopsychologies opened up the incalculable privilege of knowing that "personal" tribulations and oases of "inner" health reflect those of the world reaching around and below to within. This hardy, courageous, and often joyful knowing could pass for a workable definition of wisdom, which perhaps is another word for human maturity at its unenclosed ripest.

Foregrounding Terra

Nevertheless, a lingering disconnection continued between the unheard "sound" or "sense" of place and the human researcher's point of view. As creative as they often were, ecopsychological responses to the world's doings have tended (although not always!) to stay safely on our side of the human-nonhuman divide, still keeping us from enlisting the world as a full research partner. Books, papers, and lectures went deep into what we could make of the land—dump, parking lot, game preserve, wilderness area—but too seldom into *what the land made of us*, let alone on whether we were acting out its past and present sufferings unconsciously. Too often our wanderings about the territory made no place for the muffled voice of Terra.

Raising this concern among elite ecological thinkers can trigger an exasperating deluge in which "alterities" and "subalterns," "imbrications" and "morphogenic fields," bob like the remnants of an intellectual shipwreck. Streams of such irrelevancies gradually made it obvious that even those who care deeply about healing our relationship with Earth are liable to wield concepts defensively to smother how moved we are by the numinous power of place. In fact, most or all of the classic Freudian defenses—intellectualization, reaction-formation, denial, etc.—seem to be shadowed by ecological *safeguardings* (to resurrect Adler's less warlike term), which mask from consciousness how shrilly our very bones vibrate to the pain of the land.

In time, however, this highly abstract philosophizing felt like discussing a history of ideas under the roof of a burning building. "Intertextual multivocalities" would never put out those world-consuming flames without relevant, if imprecise, constructs that would have impact, carry weight, foment change, suggest novel directions for further inquiry. We already know that our industrially and religiously tainted relationship to our habitat is one of corrosive dissociation. To inquire from a more interior-metaphoric standpoint: Who will finally ask what the *world* does about this relationship, and how it lets us know? When will the progression outward from intrapsychic systems to family systems to ecosystems at last be complemented by a similar progression in our explorations of subjectivity from personal and social psyche to the psyche of the planet?

Terrapsychology begins with registering the *pain* (cognate to the Sanskrit *cayate*, "to take revenge") of place (*dolor loci*) echoing into conflicts and symptoms and repeating pathologies treated as purely personal, only to remain stubbornly uncured by personalistic, literalistic methods of healing. This should be expected if the wounds found all around the industrially crucified world play the same local tones as the wounds in the heart.

In a society composed of mature individuals—in other words, of interdependent, strong-hearted people not taught from the cradle to be easily distracted and wastefully uncaring—it would go without saying that polluting, paving over, and sucking resources from the land like hungry infants at the breast unroll a long list of life-threatening consequences too dangerous to entertain even in the short term. For deep ecology, this immaturity prevents empathizing with the woes of the declining natural world. But visualizing these psychological shortcomings only as barriers discounts how, there in the widening gap between the numb disconnect of normality and the ecstasy of a Muir or a Thoreau, all the stubborn greeds and meannesses, all the inconvenient hatreds and sorrows, the political hearts and economic wants rumble back and forth between person and place to bring forth treasure beyond inconvenient rips in a potential sense of oneness. For these troublesome knots and tangles weave their way down into the world's very depths.

Terrapsychology's chief task is to unroll some of this shimmering intersubjective fabric for human appreciation, reverence, and repair. Under the shadow of the empires over matter, it unraveled here and there, and psychologies that would veil it crumple it in places; but its bonds, though strained and tangled, have held. What is needed, and what follows, is a method for smoothing out some of the knots while respecting the weight and integrity of the weave.

SECTION II

Terra Firma: Amplifying the
Voice of Locale

My mother tells the story of my birth, of how, for a significant and ominous period after my delivery I did not emit a sound or show any sign of life. An old woman, an accomplished healer, was summoned. I was rushed to the family ancestral shrine, *Togbuizikpuixo* at Weta in the southern Volta Region of Ghana. It was there I came to life.

—Kofi Awoonor

CHAPTER THREE

Terrapsychology: Ancestry, Premises, and Goals

> Plants are credited with but dim and uncertain sensation, and minerals with positively none at all. But why may not even a mineral arrangement of matter be endowed with sensation of a kind that we in our blind exclusive perfection can have no manner of communication with?
>
> —John Muir, *A Thousand-Mile Walk to the Gulf*

A primary purpose of *terrapsychology*—from *terra* (Earth, ground), *psyche* (soul, mind) and *-logy* (study of)—is to tend to the psyche or soul of story-, dream-, and symptom-gathering places and their features by hearing, reflecting deeply on, and replying to their nonverbal-symbolic modes of address. This emphasis complements psychology, ecopsychology, environmental science, and mainstream ecology by responding to the terrain and its animated resonations dancing in the psychological field as reactive outer *and* inner presences with needs of their own. The terrapsychological approach explores how *the inner connection between people and planet remains active and highly resonant, providing a means to greet the* genius loci *on its own lively ground.*

In terrapsychology done well, the pathological stance of man against the elements gives way to a disciplined willingness to be mentored by them—

interaction by heartfelt interaction—without splitting the metaphoric from the tangible or the imaginal from physical. Our inquiry keeps an eye on the features from which the *genius loci* emerges into the foreground.

TERRAPSYCHOLOGY'S CULTURAL ANCESTRY

The idea that things and places possess purpose, animation, or symbolic meaning goes far back in recorded history and even beyond. It was predominant all over the globe until the ideology of the "empire of matter," described in Chapter 1, superseded it in the expanding "First" World.

- Many indigenous cultures experience the world as the living abode of a deity such as Changing Woman, the Diné (Navajo) personification of the Earth.
- For the Western Apache, locales are aware of the human activity that takes place in them and deserve great respect, which is reflected in their elaborately situational namings.[1]
- Aristotle believed things to be actuated by their own *telos* or inbuilt purpose. Steering a course between the atomistic materialism of Democritus and the otherworldliness of Plato, he thought of matter and even the universe itself as a vast unfolding from potentiality to actuality.
- The Greeks and Romans of old experienced each stream, grove, forest, mountain, and city as inhabited by its resident spirit, its *genius loci*. Every pre-industrial culture knows similar figures. A handful of examples from Europe include the Yarthings and Hyter Sprites out of Anglican folklore, the Doire well guardians of Celtic mythology, and the following pairings: dryads with trees, naiads with springs, oreads with hills and rocks, nereids, mermaids, sirens, and oceanids with the sea, and trolls and gnomes with caves. Wishing wells and coins placed in new cornerstones recall the desire to propitiate such beings.
- Neoplatonic writings mention an *anima mundi* or World Soul, an idea brought back to life by Jung and elaborated in the work of James Hillman and Robert Sardello. *Anima mundi* is a Neoplatonic counterpart to the Gnostic figure of Sophia, the divine personification of creative Wisdom.

- The alchemists, who strove to transmute base metals like lead into silver and gold, believed in what Marie-Louise von Franz referred to as divine power in matter.[2] The all-curing "Philosopher's Stone" of alchemy, for which they sweated over bubbling retorts, appeared in their fantasies as a spirit trapped in their sizzling concoctions.
- Goethe used an observational discipline akin to what would eventually be called "phenomenology" to experience an imagistic flow of becoming in the plants he studied.
- Schopenhauer argued that the everyday world of representation had a lining of "will," an inner life that infuses all that is.[3]
- Spinoza believed that a mental attribute or quality permeated existence.[4]
- The school of *Naturphilosophie* burgeoned with German Romanticism, Idealism, and the philosophical musings of Schelling mixed with those of Hegel. One of its goals was the reweaving of natural-world roots in human thought and aspiration. Schelling in particular intuited what he saw as comparisons between the evolution of human thought and nature's continuing creativity. For him, the natural and the spiritual were different ways of observing the same unitary process ultimately inaccessible to reduction as an object of intellectual knowledge.
- Jesuit scientist and scholar Teilhard de Chardin proposed a "within" of things, arguing that everything—a hillside, a stone, a piece of paper—has an objective face and a subjective face, an outer side and an inner.[5] The more complex the nervous system it possesses, the more conscious the subjectivity or interiority can be of itself. This concept philosophically subverts both the mind-body "problem" and the elusive threshold between the living and the non-living, which for him was not an either-or but a matter of degree. A cat exhibits a more complex inner life than a rock, but both possess one as a property inherent in every type of matter. For Teillard de Chardin, nothing was unalive.
- In some sects of Buddhism, things considered in the West to be inanimate, such as minerals, are seen as endowed with a

living "Buddha nature," an attitude that has worked its way into the field of deep ecology and its goal of Self-realization.

- Shinto religion offers imagistically elaborate descriptions of local *kami* (gods).
- Nineteenth-century proponents of *panpsychism*, the belief that qualities of mindfulness do not restrict themselves to human brains, include Gustav Fechner, William James, Wilhelm Wundt, Rudolf Hermann Lotze, William Clifford, Friedrich Paulsen, Morton Prince, Ferdinand Schiller, Josiah Royce, Ernst Häckel, who coined the term "ecology," and Eduard von Hartmann, among the first to write about the unconscious.[6]
- Extending the findings of the Gestaltists (Wertheimer, Koffka, and Kohler) of the 1920s, social psychologist Kurt Lewin applied their field orientation to human relationships, demonstrating how features of the immediate environment acquire psychologically symbolic values that interact dynamically within the psychological field. This field, which Lewin called the "life space," organized inner and outer interactions into a unified psychological whole of the kind described by later psychoanalysts and Gestalt psychotherapists.
- The depth psychology tradition rooted in these ancient philosophies and inaugurated by Pierre Janet, Sigmund Freud, and C. G. Jung, and further extended by James Hillman and Robert Sardello, imagines consciousness as situated upon a primary process or substrate of fantasy, image, and myth that informs every realm of human experience (e.g., the computer as a return of the mythic figure of the robotic Golem). Irreducible to neurochemistry and resistant to literalization or centralized ego control, this polycentric language or layer of being can be approached, like the presence of place, only in terms of its own mythopoetic movements—movements which exist *prior* to thought and reflection, like a shimmer of myth already at work under everything we perceive and categorize.
- The practice of discerning the consistency and order structuring these symbolisms as they unfold in the animated world is as old as art, ritual, sacred dance, and dream interpretation. The

intuitively felt "aha!" connection valued by all the deep psychologies—psychoanalytic, humanistic, existential, Jungian—represents a valid and highly reliable internal shift in understanding, not a calculable proof. "The autonomy of fantasy is the soul's last refuge of dignity, its guarantor against all oppressions; it alone we can take with us into the barracks behind the barbed wire. If we are willing to accept internal controls upon the imagination, we will have succumbed already in soul to the same authoritarianism that would dominate the body politic."[7] And the body of Earth as part of the same program.

- Jung tried his own hand at tending the imaginal dimension of matter:

> The psyche, if you understand it as a phenomenon occurring in living bodies, is a quality of matter, just as our body consists of matter. We discover that this matter has another aspect, namely, a psychic aspect. It is simply the world seen from within. It is just as though you were seeing into another aspect of matter. This is an idea that is not my invention. Old Democritus talked of the 'spiritus insertus atomis,' the spirit inserted in atoms. That means the psyche is a quality which appears in matter.[8]

- Jung also pointed out that the unconscious tends to behave toward us in step with how we treat it.[9] Repress its impulses and they resurface as symptoms, unexpected moods, nightmares, explosions of anger, physical ailments. When heeded, its voices and figures are less likely to possess the conscious mind, or to trip it up from within its blind spots. Throughout his *Collected Works* one finds repeated his idea that the reactive human unconscious ultimately merges with the world.
- Ecofeminist Stephanie Lahar argues that subjectivity is not limited to humanity; rather, human consciousness is but one specialized form of a subjectivity found throughout the natural world.[10]
- Environmental researcher Val Plumwood favors an "intentional panpsychism," which avoids the on-off, "it-is-or-it-isn't" mode of thinking about consciousness:

> The rich intentionality the reductive stance would deny
> to the world is the ground of the enchantment it retains
> in many indigenous cultures and in some of the past of
> our own, the butterfly wing-dust of wonder that
> modernity stole from us and replaced with the drive
> for power.[11]

- Along with practitioners of the Chinese art of *feng shui*, or the beneficial alignment of human structures with their geographical locations, examples of contemporary artists who take the presence of place seriously include landscape designer Lawrence Halprin, known to camp out at a site of future building in order to study the lay and feel of the place; sculptor Andy Goldsworthy, who considers his projects of root, stone, leaf, and ice to be gifts to the place where he creates them; and the groups of muralists, dancers, writers, and dramatists who make the border between Mexico and the United States part of their performances.

Terrapsychology seeks to value this animistic tradition by seeing the spirit of place as a kind of outward interiority, an inner life of things in the world. To do this it entertains a set of provisional ideas that guide its attempts to listen in on locale.

Premises of Terrapsychology

Terrapsychology's working premises include the following:

1. Interiority (inwardness, subjectivity, the inner life) reaches wider and deeper than electrochemical activity in people's heads. It is more like a dimension or field of being. Whatever resides in the psychological field carries aspects of interiority.

2. The nonhuman world partakes of this interiority in ways we do not really understand but can verify experientially. We can make use of the inner pole of our subjectivity to detect what manifest as animated subjectivities that haunt the places where we live because these qualities of animation interact with us psychically in a charged interactive field of continual dialog. In other words, places approach us through

symbols that connect us to them. Those most sensitive to human interference carry the highest psychic charge.

3. Although these largely unnoticed interactions go on all the time, we miss them because the self-world split endemic to Western culture renders place-personifications in dreams, recurrent local motifs, and other parallels between the personal/inner and ecological/outer invisible, particularly when psychology relegates them entirely to the human interior. When wounds, misfortunes, or weaknesses are constellated by traumas going on around us, we tend to focus on personal woes without seeing the larger themes behind them.

4. These patterns of interaction between people and places are arrestingly consistent, symbolically rich, and thematically meaningful. For example, wild bears have recently wandered into the hospital emergency rooms of at least two heavily industrialized nations. The bears join many other endangered creatures that have been forced by us into the "emergency room" phase of their survival, like the deer that was literally "caught in the headlights" while running across the Golden Gate Bridge. From the literalist perspective, such incursions probably reflect the growing intrusion of urbanization into formerly wild areas. Seen symbolically, they seem like gestures, responses, or even instinctive protests.

5. Nature turns toward us the face that we turn toward it. Regard it as raw material and it will ignite our symptoms; ignore its history and its trauma will historicize ours; relegate it to inferiority, and it will find basements in life for us to stumble into or attics to topple from. (Winnicott's description of how the neuroses of parents can "impinge" dangerously on a child's mind[12] could be widened to include the environment's unheeded inner voice speaking loudly through human conflict.)

6. Repression of the sense of place or commodification of a landscape by turning it into an ideology (as in patriotically touted nationalism or "blood-and-soil" collective narcissism) results in the negative projection of earthiness onto people regarded as Other: those seen as animalistic, bestial, "children of nature," primitive, savage, or otherwise subhuman.

7. Aspects of ongoing person-place interactions can be interpreted if we allow a place and its occupants to "speak" to us, in effect treating it like a piece of internal psychic structure. Taking the presence of place on its own interior terms includes holding, hearing, and making room for its untold histories much as a psychotherapist provides a living receptacle for taking in the client's intolerable emotional states, digesting them, and giving them back in manageable portions.[13]

8. When we listen to the presence of place, the place may stop impinging and "speak" more softly as person-place dialogs diminish the overidentification inherent in repressing environmental presences. Nightmares soften into dreams, repetitions into reworkings of old themes, inner pressure into advocacy, accidents into encounters. Nature-themed projections onto marginalized groups of people diminish. All this suggests that:

9. Places make use of their relationship with us to reorganize themselves (and us) inwardly and outwardly. The nature and extent of reorganization is not yet understood, but it seems to involve a stabilizing, strengthening, or enrichment of the *genius loci*.

10. If carefully attended to, this continual dialog informs the ecological structuring of enduring human communities in which people remember how to experience themselves not as autonomous egos but more naturally, as indigenous openings or nodes of contact with each other and the environment.

These assumptions support a burgeoning field of reflective inquiry whose prototype research method, Terrapsychological Inquiry, is explained in Chapters 4 and 5. The field's areas of focus[14] are described in the following shorthand:

- Archetypal geography (Chapter 6): the study of the relationship between locale and its animate mythology.
- Dialogical alchemy (Chapter 7): a continuation of the alchemist's search for the sense of animation in matter.
- Lorecasting (Chapter 8): the hermeneutic investigation of natural events such as epidemics and earthquakes in terms of their symbolic or "inner" dynamics.

- Psychocartography (Chapter 8, "Beyond This Point"): charting the psyche of place.

Not all such terrapsychological work with place need conform to specific areas of specialization or types of inquiry. In all cases the presences, features, and details under study should govern the method of study. Investigations of place vary from rigorous, thorough assessments to getting a quick sense of the *genius loci* during a short visit. Descriptions of results span the gamut from poetic to pedantic. What the methods, steps, tendings, or reflections share is an open-hearted willingness to allow the spirit of a place access to a receptive and embodied human consciousness.

Goals

The goals of a terrapsychological approach include the following:

- To learn how what appear in the psychological field as nonhuman subjectivities—geographical locales, their compositional elements, their plants and animals—address us in synchronization with how we behave toward them, with place as an orienting context.
- To add the dimension of depth to environmental and ecological studies by perceiving features of the terrain, as much as can be done, from the inside, in terms (to put it poetically) of how they seem to themselves.
- To explore the inner/symbolic meaning of the worldwide indigenous certainty that places are animated by living forces. As Thoreau put it, there is no such thing as "inorganic" in such a framework.
- To make these forces visible, particularly when they resurface in human psychological life, cultural activity, bodily states, and unconscious repetitions of local historical events.
- To demonstrate the unbreakable interdependency between psychological health, social justice, and ecological well-being.
- To challenge healing modalities such as psychotherapy to return to the native sensibility that possibilities for health and illness are not separate from where they are seen.

- To make more apparent and less confining the unconscious identity that binds us to environmental forces and features, and thereby enlarge both our sense of identity and our feeling of partnership with the nonhuman.
- To create ideas and practices which encourage *deep heartsteading*: dwelling deeply in places through knowledge and love that strengthen over time in continual interactions between the human and the nonhuman.

From the human side of the apparent gap between self and world, terrapsychological methods seek to amplify the nonhuman voices that cross it like sparks leaping a synapse, thereby narrowing the ancient gulf behind so much misery and destruction, one mindful dialog at a time. At bottom, terrapsychology is a tending of the mindfulness of all things insofar as they address us.

Because the most ecologically wounded locales tend to emanate the clearest signals, an obvious way to start is by unpacking Terrapsychological Inquiry, our "psychoanalysis of place."

CHAPTER FOUR

Reading the Woes of the World

If the earth is something more than inert matter whirling through space, perhaps in some sense alive, how would it communicate that to us? What would our antennae pick up?

—David Orr, *Listening to the Land*

Terrapsychological Inquiry (formerly referred to as "the locianalytic method" and "locianalysis," named in honor of the *genius loci*; hereafter abbreviated to "TI"[1]) begins with the recognition that *places behave as though they possess an imaginal interactivity or "presence" that reflects what was done to them and upon them, and they communicate this to their inhabitants and investigators through dreams, trauma, folklore, and replays of unhealed past events*. That is how psychological symptoms work too. What, after all, is an unresolved injury but a body of history repressed into voicelessness?

In this chapter and those following appear a number of techniques for getting closer to the soul of a locale: for example, asking the locale for dreams, studying its history and ecology, comparing the motifs of one's personal biography to those inhabiting the environment, keeping track of moods felt in different spots, visiting sacred sites, using ceremonial practices. Still under development, the intersubjective method of inquiry outlined below is intended only as a blueprint for using these techniques in a research context. As with any sustainable dwelling, the blueprint should always be made to conform to the terrain.

TERRAPSYCHOLOGICAL ASSESSMENT: HOW TO APPROACH THE TERRAIN

Attentiveness to potential signals of storied traumas locked in place is the move suggested by TI, a method by which the presence of a place—including its shadow, as Jung would say: the side of it farthest from the daylight of community consciousness—is amplified through a systematic examination of its history, legends, dreams, pathologies, and other markers of stirred psychic life as they develop against the movements and contours of the land. Listening in on damaged locales, like a therapist resonating to a client's deepest wounding, the method requires a bracketing of the cultural bias against the world's aliveness, a willingness to seek out meaningful alignments of external and internal events, an imaginative use of one's subjectivity to detect the feel or sense of place, and a working familiarity with that place's history, geography, and ecological health. Without these attitudes, the approach will have no greater success than treating a patient like a corpse, only to wonder at the absence of any signs of life.

Because terrapsychology holds the presence of place as a "reconciling third" between its objective and subjective aspects, TI makes use of research procedures traditionally categorized as both qualitative and quantitative. The first come more finely tuned for experiential work and less apt to contaminate the research with Cartesian-Newtonian defenses of distancing and reductionism. The second remind us that what we study wears an outer face too.

The inquiry into place breaks down into two overlapping stages: *assessment*, described in this chapter, and *placehosting,* described in Chapter 5. In some ways the method parallels general psychotherapeutic practice, with the researcher as therapist, the place as client, and stories of trauma awaiting the hearing that will let them conclude.

PREPARATION PHASE

In entering these localized fields and their powerful inductions, the key facilitative attitude is one of *sensitized innocence,* an openness that willingly suspends ingrained prejudices long enough for the individual or team to offer sufficient psychological space for whatever the place under study might reveal. This type of openness grounds itself in the following activities:

1. "Reading" the terrain with an awareness that bounces back and forth between movements in the environment and movements within.
2. Allowing questions to receive more attention than answers.
3. Giving imaginings priority over preconceptions.
4. Holding the body in attention as an important way to discover where the place and self poles of the interactive field overlap.
5. *Honoring active associations*—those that bubble forth imaginatively from a particular feature of the terrain—as potential ecological indicators.[2]
6. Being receptive to fresh impressions that swarm into the foreground as bits of knowledge (local history, climate, infrastructure, etc.) recede for a time into the background.
7. Conceptualizing every aspect of the interchange between the witness and the witnessed, the hearer and the heard, as dialogical, as persons and places sharing psyche.
8. Employing a *nomadic awareness* that sets aside the habit of seeing the land through the cracked lens of ownership or appropriation in order to follow its lead through a series of intimate contacts and relinquishments.[3]

ASSESSMENT PHASE

How the assessment unfolds depends on the subject of the inquiry, whether a city, a mythic figure such as Prometheus who appears often in Switzerland, a rockslide that closes off the main road to ecologically stressed Yosemite, or a tsunami that obliterates a key east-west trade route. Because the most involved inquiry involves hunting for recurring motifs in a particular landscape, that type will furnish the example below.

The first three assessment items—Locale, Infrastructure, and Community—provide a *place history*, the terrapsychological equivalent of the case history of psychotherapy. The fourth, Genius Loci, draws on this information to sift out the recurrent themes and images that paint in the presence of the spirit or soul of place.

The Four Domains

1. Locale

The locale is the physical configuration and dimensions of the area under examination, considering, for example, past and present geographical activity; local watersheds, deserts, mountains, minerals and resources, soil types, ecosystems; local ecological concerns and what, if anything, is being done about them; flora and fauna, and what is happening to their diversity; climate and weather patterns; natural disasters; outstanding features. A factual history of the place should be conducted for as far back in time as can be accomplished (see the work of John Mitchell[4] for an instructive example of how to do this) as well as giving particular notice to features undergoing shifts, like fault line movements, extended droughts, replacement of original plants by invasive species, snowpack breakups. The idea is to form an impression of the nonhuman aspects of the site both before and after its inhabitation.

2. Infrastructure

The infrastructure consists of human-built components: key industries and their impact on the environment, origin and impact of water, energy, sewage management, and garbage disposal, traffic patterns, transportation pathways (the place's arteries), age and type of local architecture (its skeleton), preferred structures for power/ information/ entertainment transmission (its nerves). Anything built locally that stands out from the background is potential grist for this mill.

3. Community

The third domain to be considered in the assessment is the cultural-communal component from the place's founding to the present: ethnic groups, social justice issues, art and culture, political climate, population demographics, crime, fashion trends, typical community events, local folklore and legends, public figures, stories about the place's founding. (Note: A participatory action approach can minimize the power imbalances between the "scientific" researcher and the community by involving the community from the start, e.g., in helping formulate the research foci. At the very least the community should benefit from the results.)

4. *Genius Loci*

With locale, infrastructure, and community as its skin, bones, and organs, *the living, reactive field manifests as the imaginal presence of a particular place.* This presence appears with particular vividness in these ten spheres of experience:

- *Dreams*, especially those in which the *genius loci* appears as a person, as San Diego did in the dream described in the Introduction.
- *Actings out of local complexes, myths, repetitions, and woundings.* In the crossroads town of Sebastopol, California, for example, a Garden of Eden motif forms out of the following when considered together: a proliferation of apple images, the nearby Luther Burbank garden, the cherublike sculptures at one end of the city ("I am the Guardian of the Gate," says the plaque), unintended but plentiful sacrificial offerings of animals (including snakes) struck by cars, and other Edenic themes echoing forth as residents turn out time and again in wrap skirts and sandals for organic festivals echoing themes out of Genesis.[5]
- *Placefield motifs*, the recurring themes shared by people and places alike, are to a place what character patterns and long-standing self structures are to a human personality. In Escondido, California, for example, a place once called the Devil's Corner and sold in the 1800s as a rancho for $666.66, the motifs of Hiddenness and Visibility alternate across the decades and throughout the city in many different manifestations. Examples of the Hiddenness motif include the city's name ("hidden" in Spanish), the hidden Escondida River flowing underground (but represented somehow on the map of explorer Juan Bautista Anza), vanished veins of gold, Californio troops hidden by fog during the Battle of San Pasqual, three concealed American scouts who left the battlefield afterward, and the field itself, as yet unlocated. Examples of the Visibility motif include the first trains through named One-Eyed Monsters, the "Giant Eye" telescope at Palomar, a popular local romance penned by an optician, and

a story of an Indian about to shoot his wife from jealousy until he saw the act imaged on a nearby rock. *The more often and peculiarly such motifs recur, the more boldy they stand out from the background and the stronger the sense that their repetition signals an important underlying presence.*

- Placefield motifs are like personality quirks. *Placefield syndromes* are its complexes. They indicate where the aliveness of the location being studied is most discounted by its human population. They are where the place is most pathologized and most strenuously insists on its animated presence. A motif such as Visibility takes on fresh meaning through ongoing incidents of conjunctivitis, missing glasses, and broken mirrors.

- *Historically significant figures* whose biographies often burst with symptomatic themes (e.g., John Muir's heart giving out with that of the engineer who flooded Hetch Hetchy; both men died not long after the dam's aortic pumps put the valley's heart underwater).

- *Local news and past and recent events.* What is buried resurfaces, like the Chumash bones that pop up periodically in the carefully cultivated gardens of Mission Santa Barbara, or the pans and pickaxes that shoot up out of golf courses during earthquakes in San Francisco. Recurring local themes reanimate Cortez in our complexes, civil wars in St. Louis, fountains of youth in Florida.

- *Local folklore*, including legends, tales, ghost sightings, stories handed down, etc., can yield clues about placefield motifs. La Llorona, the ghostly Weeping Woman of Mexican legend, has been known to cry out in places undergoing overdevelopment.[6] Some version of her haunts every Mission county in California as her sisters walk the night in Arizona, New Mexico, and Texas. Folklore is at least in part the dream of place and can be listened into as such. Ignored, it becomes dangerously, possessively re-enacted, as when psychotic mothers married to mythic Jasons or living in overdeveloped areas drown their children and cry out like La Llorona without ever knowing they have repeated a tragic regional tale.[7]

- Local *architecture and art*—murals, paintings, drama, music, sculpture, abstract art—sift place-embedded themes, especially those which appear in personified form like people in dreams or characters in a play. What divisions does that arch in once-divided St. Louis evoke? Why is the Golden Gate Bridge red of all colors, with engineers who survived a plunge from the pylons naming themselves the Halfway to Hell Club? Why does Mission Revival architecture spread faster than cancer? In what way do the Missions themselves ooze with the fascination of unhealed sores?

- Some places seem to be more confrontive or disturbed than others. The severity of human lovelessness and damage done to a place bears a relation to its *ecoreactivity*, the strength with which placefield themes crash into awareness there. Ecoreactivity often increases temporarily toward the investigator seeking themes and can be very dangerous, as the following chapter makes clear. (Speaking technically: the concept of the bioregion, a zone of similar ecosystems—a watershed, for example—can be supplemented with that of a *psychoregion* corresponding to a mapped and inhabited area like a city or a county. It may be that a given community is psychologically and ecologically stable only to the degree that its psychoregion and bioregion align with one another.)

- *Ecotransference* is the sum of unintegrated emotional reactions to the characteristics of the place under investigation. These reactions always carry an unconscious component normally tied to woundings in the investigator. The presence of an unconscious identification with a place or some aspect of it distinguishes ecotransference from empathy. Empathy with a troubled place can hurt, but ecotransference hooks the empathizer by the unconscious. Because it elicits human involvement, it furnishes a prime tool of assessment when monitored for how places trigger reactions from one's personal history, relationships, dreams, moods, physical discomforts, key conflicts, and psychological symptoms as they surface in that locale, just as the psychotherapist's trained awareness floats in emotional responses and free associations that arise in the presence of the client. If possible, the researchers should record whatever dreams occur while sleeping in the area under study—a practice similar to the ancient Greek ritual of asking for dreams in the temples of healing—as well as the dreams of any family members, friends, colleagues, or loved ones present in the same setting at the time of investigation. However, seeking parallels between dream images and local themes must not degenerate into the deanimating "naturalistic fallacy"[8] of *reducing* images to soils or seas and thereby subordinating the presence of the place to its material features. A horse "dreamed" locally might resemble a horse stabled nearby, but both say more as emplaced imaginal gestures or movements than if either were *explained* in terms of the other.

Emplaced Motifs and the Genius Loci

A person obsessed with knives, spears, deflated balloons, pincushions, tacks, and pokers could easily be identified as preoccupied with *Penetration*, but recurrent motifs are often easier to spot in people than in places—even in Pan-haunted Escondido, where the safety pin and horseshoe nail originated as part of a local history of drilling, lancing, cruising, and sperm-bank-aided reproduction, human and animal. How do we tell when we have found such motifs?

1. They recur too often, too predictably, and too symbolically to be attributed to mere coincidence, except when squeezed into the most reductive of conceptual frameworks.

2. They radiate into not one or two, but many domains of experience, including ecology, architecture, biography, politics, civic planning, local history, and personal psychology.

3. They possess enormous transgressive power, easily crossing boundaries from land to art, from dream to ambition, from earth to sky.

4. The peer support and wisdom that should accompany the entire assessment can pause here to offer critical feedback. Questions they

should ponder include: Does the researcher really have a sense of the place? Are the motif recurrences frequent, and do the interpretations flow integrally from them or seem more like researcher projections obscuring the landscape, physical or imaginal? Do other researchers confirm the impressions so far? What personal conflicts or wounds are being triggered? What might help more effectively manage the ecotransference? Are there signs of placefield traumas leaking into the researcher's home life, relationships, career, physical or mental health? (If so, the study should be suspended until they are adequately managed and the unconscious over-identification rendered transparent.) What are the strengths and weaknesses of the assessment thus far, and of what the researcher plans for the phases that follow?

5. Placefield motifs remain intensely *local* even while drawing material from outside the region.

6. The motifs cannot be accounted for as socially handed-down tales or legends. Residents new or old would have to somehow learn of them, consciously or unconsciously, in order to repeat them, and this is not the case. Nor can this kind of cultural diffusion explain ecoreactive manifestations like symbolically significant dust storms blowing in just when a curious observer enters a city that the desert fights to reclaim for itself. Once this has happened repeatedly, the impression that places do not wait passively to be attended to is hard to avoid. Sooner or later, dreams and themes underline the location's *ecological* malaise. The impression of wounds being turned toward the observer is unmistakable.

7. Their tremendous reactivity responds directly to the researcher's thoughts, moods, and actions, *like dreams correcting a misinterpreted symbol from a previous dream.* (While investigating Escondido, I had only to wonder about the pitchfork/penetration motif to find my car and bicycle tires flattened. In the trunk of a used car I bought I found a toy cavalry sword. On one such occasion a bee flew into my mouth.)

8. Taken together, they express various facets of a self-consistent *central image* embedded in the place from which it seeps into the sphere of human experience. This image is the *genius loci* proper, the spirit or soul of the place.

Like its placefield manifestations, the central image of a locale, animated so vividly there in the psychological field, cannot be reduced to a human projection—even ignoring the fact that projections as clinically understood emanate primarily from psychopathology—because it always displays geographical and ecological roots and features of the terrain. With its fiery dryness, its knack for urban self-renewal, and its veins of tributary streams reaching out from the city like opening wings, Phoenix consistently presents itself as phoenix-like across nonhuman as well as human dimensions, just as castles nestled into Santa Barbara's coastal peaks both recall the high tower from which Saint Barbara gazed down upon the villagers below. Like a psychological complex or a long-standing trait of character, the *genius loci* finds many ways to express its particular style.

Rather than reducing a place or theme to human projection, it makes better sense to think of the central image of a locale, around which so much imagery and recurring narrative turn, as a place's inner being or picture of itself: its essence sensed from within. In the field between itself and its occupants, its image comes vividly to life, expressing itself beneficially when respected and loved, and violently when diminished by thoughtless human influence.

Assessments can be complex, but the rationale is rather simple. The main points are to study the surround and its history, to research community happenings, to start looking for suggestive images and themes that indicate points of recurrent trauma, to host them via the psychological field, and *to find ways to allow them to deepen beyond their appearance as random-seeming events.* They usually will not be difficult to find. The record of transportation in Peter Pan-like Santa Cruz, perennial site of lofty Divine Child accelerations, looks like a case history of crashes and reckless driving. Towers have been falling in once-forested Manhattan, New York City, whose motto is *Excelsior* ("Ever Upward"), since the collapsed Dutch fort whose stones went home as souvenirs. Romulus and Remus still live in Rome in robes resembling priestly vestments worn in mythic times gone by.

Alonzo Horton, future founder of the American version of San Diego, was visiting Panama one day in 1856 when a mob stormed the hotel where he and his fellow cruise ship passengers were staying as honored guests. Firing his revolver in lethal self-defense, he retreated with a tight knot of escapees up the gangplank, only to realize he had left $10,000 in gold dust behind. Too late to return for it. He was lucky to escape with his life.

The incident as stated means little enough; but not far to the north, another band of enterprising travelers had been attacked by a mob of angry locals three centuries earlier. Caught by surprise, the frightened party of formerly honored guests had retreated up a gangway while firing at its onrushing assailants, killing some. Left behind: a pile of gold, lost in the heat of a frantic retreat. Like Horton, their leader would eventually found a sprawling city on the ruins of a once-beautiful expanse of land and water, would destroy what was there to do it, would swell with money and fame for a time, would lose both, and would die in relative poverty. That his name was also that of Horton's ship capped the echo's uncanny exactness: the *Cortez*.

Coincidence? Or are such replays—in this case one would-be empire-builder deaf to his surroundings made to follow unconsciously in the footsteps of another—more frequent than is commonly realized, particularly in locations subject to conquest and the heavy building that follows? *Does the story of what traumatized the land keep repeating until finally heard and healed?* In Mexico City, which the Americans occupied during the Mexican War, General William Worth held a puzzlingly irrational belief that, like Cortez, he was vastly outnumbered by the enemy forces around him. This fear prompted him to change his brigade's quarters several times, from near the plaza where the Aztec imperial compound had stood to the western entrance, and then to the east, a series of moves that roughly traced the conquistadors' march into the area, but in reverse. Not long after this bizarre reprisal, General Winfield Scott invaded Mexico's interior with a force far less than that of his enemies. He used no fixed base of operations, kept the defenders retreating, stormed their entrenchments, captured the capital, and conquered the government in a second symbolic fall of the Aztec capital.

Symptoms and syndromes of place go on and on and relentlessly on from within as well as without, breaking hearts, amplifying obsessions, erupting in civic political battles between mysteriously enraged opponents. They shout, scream, rumble, and bleed until they get a hearing. Providing a hearing for them is a key aim of assessment.

When untended, these pernicious influences steepen exponentially over time into more and more dire repercussions concatenating through the local human-nature community. Fortunately, so does the kind of healing that addresses the damaging misalignment between inner and outer inherent in empire's attack upon the world and, by extension, upon human sanity.

There is a language beyond human language, an elemental language, one that rises from the land itself.

—Linda Hogan

CHAPTER FIVE

Tending Reactive Terrain

It is no mere coincidence that our feelings about a place take on spiritual dimensions. An old rancher once told me he thought the lines in his hand had come directly up from the earth, that the land had carved them there after so many years of work.

—Gretel Ehrlich, "Landscape"

As a wordlessly traumatized survivor symbolically retells his tale through his symptoms, or a badly frightened animal reinvents its terror in later encounters by snarling reactively at those who approach, so do injured landscapes induce their themes and anguishes in us, tingeing the interactive field with placefield images of their sufferings.

Ongoing parallels between their stories and ours unfold as we stand in their presence to make this once-disregarded connection evident.

PLACEHOSTING PHASE

The assessment described in the preceding chapter initiates a careful, multileveled, and multidisciplinary tending of the ignored or silenced "voice" of place and the beginning of an ecological empathy between us and our surroundings.

Placehosting deepens the encounter between the locale and us by shifting from the overall diagnostic outline of the place's key points of anguish into an imaginative, open-hearted, and ceremonial-communal mode of personal *response* brought back to the locale and the community.

There are more ways to placehost than can be dreamed of within the circumference of one book, for here the creative powers of the researcher come fully into their own. Giving expression to buried stories emanating from the land—not to rewrite them but to let them finish themselves—can prove particularly healing for everyone and everything concerned. Three key questions guide this stage of the work: What does the place want from me? What obligations has it left me with? How effectively can I stay with and tend the potent actuality I sense here instead of escaping into some kind of treatment plan imposed from above?

"Ethics" derives from *ethos*, which in Homer's time meant an animal habitat, such as the place where wild horses go to rest for the night, and the word, therefore, carries ecological implications.[1] Terrapsychology views the sense of ethical responsibility as an active, affirmative power that expresses itself first by refusing to ignore wounded locales and their suffering communities, and then by responding from the *heart*, the psychic core of the researcher, where introversion changes into extraversion and back again in a heartbeat. Moved and enlarged, the heart as emotive analogue of the researcher's psychological depth and harborer of ecological reveries indicates the choice of interventions, like a weather vane swinging to a moisture-laden breeze.

Placehosting might include sharing findings with the local community, discussing the methodology with students, rousing resistance to the encroachment of land-gulping "development," ecological grief work of the kind conducted by Joanna Macy,[2] educating the public about the local dangers of pollution, even painting the dangers in an evocative public mural. A woman possessed of a ceremonial bent sang to her ranch while walking its perimeter; another made use of the guerrilla gardening technique of planting to rejuvenate an abandoned field. In Santa Cruz, the San Lorenzo River Institute taught children to sample the river's waters to track fluctuations in its health. As many possibilities for response await as there are places to respond to. However, to truly host place these would need to address the relationship between the *genius loci* and its symbolic connections to the inner life of the inhabitants: monitoring of emotional rivers in parallel with the San Lorenzo, gardening as a mutuality of personal and vegetative growth, images of *earthly* grieving, activism in the spirit as well as the contours of a threatened plot of land. Above all, placehostings should spring from the felt demands of places, never from improvement programs imposed primarily from the realm of human ego. In fact, to the degree placehosting faithfully follows the inner and outer contours of the terrain, it bypasses the ego-realm literalisms of environmental science or activism as normally performed in order to be mentored by what the terrain seems to want of us. Places are active partners, not passive patients whose health status we know better than they do.

Extremes of response not geared to the spirit of the place jeopardize the internal spaces of reflection needed for the work. Probing the hurt of any overdeveloped or otherwise injured location is liable to bring up intense anger, a natural reaction; but crossing the line into violent protest, vandalism, or *ecotage*—destroying the machinery that grinds up the aching ground—runs the risk of overidentifying with a place to the extent of perpetuating harm and injustice. Asked how she could treat so many suffering people, a therapist colleague had this to say: "I have gone home thinking about my clients, empathizing with their pain, and even crying with them when it felt appropriate to; but it would help no one to drown in the same pool with them." This is advice worth following outdoors in interacting with a locale as a patient.

Mutual Deepenings

A heartfelt dynamic common to all forms of placehosting might be described as a *deepening* of the kind that envisions localized statistics, themes, histories, facts, and pathologies as symbols, images, and signals that carry forward and punctuate the stories places seem to breathe. Bringing the discussion of soul back into psychology, James Hillman describes "soul-making" as an imaginative activity in which events deepen into experiences.[3] Similarly, the shifting, grinding continent's edge that outlines the West Coast of North America dreams itself into many imaginings in the heart of the reflective witness standing with his back to the mainland as the sun falls seaward: runs and plays on at-the-edge possibility, jagged splits, collisions both civic and psychic, plate-tectonic metaphors growing social conflict and psychological upheaval reminiscent of more than a million years of rising coastal mountains eroded by currents running hot and cold ….

Deepenings help polish placefield syndromes into motifs while uncovering their intricate connections to the genius loci *from which they originally emanate and the human realm into which they radiate.* Psychologically, symptoms announce voices excluded from what should be a democracy of self where everyone speaks.[4] Ecologically, voices of the land excluded from civic planning in Phoenix overrun the grids: instead of flights of fancy and sky-watching parties, fumes from broken wine bottles and smoky currents of airplane noise tacking across Sky Harbor. And is it any wonder moods go up and down along streets cut to run straight up hillsides, as they do in San Francisco, instead of winding naturally around them? In the symptom waits the spirit of place seeking its wings in reflective appreciation. At the community level, this could show up in higher "flights" and fewer jets, or retrofits giving way phoenix-fashion to rejuvenative experiments in desert sustainability that help the place rejuvenate itself. In dreams, hostile or crazy place personifications evolve into teachers, lovers, and companions, not because the dreamer pushes for them to, but precisely because their aberrations and wailings and ragings receive full, empathic attention. The images they bring should be tended through writing, painting, ritual, slideshow, sculpture, meditation: some medium that allows them conscious actualization, personal expression, and social and psychic space in their own territory.

Deepening dovetails naturally into other kinds of reflective doing. A place might enter a dream to beckon quite directly for a particular shift of focus, or a high-energy fantasy might recur enough to suggest a new course of action on behalf of the *genius loci* animating it. Whatever the externals, and however simple or elaborate, all forms of placehosting reflectively or meditatively "dream" uncovered themes and untold stories back into their source through imaginal dialogs or ceremonial activity. From antiquity into the present, indigenous practitioners relied on shamanic[5] and other ceremonial techniques for healing damaged locales and reinvesting disrupted spots with vitality.

What does the place get out of all this effort?

PLACES RESPOND

For a long while now, an odd idea has prevailed—that the only purpose of the world is to provide local color in a divine drama staged for heaven and humans. This demotes earthly places to mere backdrops, sceneries, or resources to be dispensed with once the "real" story ends. That the world can speak or suffer, that its psychic qualities merge with our own, that humans can injure it not only physically but psychically too, or that its opening buds call out "Spring!" as in the poetry of e. e. cummings were ideas that over the centuries came to be viewed negatively as delusions, unproductive fantasies, inconvenient cows on the train tracks of progress.

Now we are learning something different. Judging by the rapidity and force of its self-disclosures in the interactive field, a world that gestures through dreams, through symptoms, through the symbolic actings out of animals and even plants, and through returns of the historically place-harming repressed is a world that wants to be heard, and wants it with such yearning that it grinds on our bones and grows weeds in our minds until we take it seriously. It was that old idealist Bishop Berkeley who summed it up so well: to be is to be perceived.

Although it will take much more research to get a sense of just how terrapsychological listenings-in affect the placefields we approach and that approach us, dreams and work in the field suggest that our tendings strengthen the spirit of particular locales, enliven their "moods," brighten their syndromes into motifs, and diminish their ecoreactivity. My own fieldwork indicates that the pathological forces that infect the locales may transform, radically; the difference in mood, feel, and reactivity after tending a place is striking. After finishing my research on San Diego, I dreamed of standing in an outdoor graduation ceremony where a smiling woman in a dark gown handed me a diploma. In the dream I understood I was being given this certificate of graduation because "UC San Diego" ("You see San Diego"). Cars do not careen toward me in Santa Cruz any more, nor do my moods swing so wildly in San Francisco, nor do I weep or vomit after passing by one of the missions. The coast of California as a whole has settled into me in step with my settlings into it. As with a series of openings outward into visibility in Escondido, haunt of the Hiddenness syndrome, shifts as obvious as key boulevards being widened and streams being cleared of invasive growth may follow the research even when not directly linked to it.

> What I have noticed in my small world is that if I praise the wild flowers growing on the hill in front of my house, the following year they double in profusion and brilliance. If I admire the squirrel that swings from branch to branch outside my window, pretty soon I have three or four squirrels to admire. If I look into the eyes of a raccoon that has awakened me by noisily rummaging through the garbage at night, and acknowledge that it looks maddeningly like a mischievous person—paws on hips, masked eyes, a certain impudent stance, as it looks back at me—I soon have a family of raccoons living in a tree a few yards off my deck. … And then, too, there are the deer, who know they need never, ever fear me.—Alice Walker, "The Universe Responds"[6]

Placehosting also encourages the dwellers in a troubled place to *reinhabit* it, as the bioregionalists like to say: to know its strengths and weaknesses, flora and fauna, growth and past intimately, as indigenous inhabitants do. Closing the unnatural gap between person and place, spirit and Earth, not only suggests new groundings for human health— physical, mental, spiritual—it transforms the compulsion to repeat, which Freud linked to self-sabotage and a hidden urge for death.[7] The strings of local history exert similarly a fatalistic-feeling drag, but like their more personalistic counterparts (e.g., one failed relationship after another), they lose their hold when sounded consciously and retreat back into the landscape.

With them vanishes much of the unconscious hatred and fear felt toward the animate world. As conflict declines on both sides of the psychological field, comprehension of deep interdependency dampens the need to continue to war against nature.

PRESENTING THE FINDINGS

Compiling and reporting on the research findings sometimes plays a part in placehosting or, in some cases, constitutes it, as when the researcher translates the results of a terrapsychological analysis into terms and images comprehensible to a community.

Presenting findings includes incubating them first to get feedback from the place where they arose, analyzing them, presenting them, and ritually closing the study.

Incubating the Findings

After all the work of assessing, hosting, dealing with ecocounter-transference, etc., a period of quiescence allows the *genius loci* time to digest the study and give the investigator some final feedback, particularly in response to the lingering question of how all this effort might have benefited the location.

Analyzing the Findings

Evaluating terrapsychological data means sifting through impressions, images, bits of local history and biography, quantitative ecological information, dream journals, somatic reactions, mood changes, animal behavior changes, and the like in search of self-storying themes. This aspect of the work is phenomenological *first*, in terms of describing experiences on location, and interpretive *second*, as the focus shifts to apprehending symbolic patternings of the data collected.[8] Identification of a motif should receive plentiful support from recurring examples of it across many domains of experience: for example, repeating instances of the "vision" or "eye" motif in Parisian art, politics, philosophy, ecology; the rotating wheel in Muscovite industry, revolution, architecture; Romulus and Remus still fighting for dominance in Rome.

At a minimum, a terrapsychological study should describe the emplaced subjectivity being studied (storms as symbolic cleansings, Los Angeles as fallen angel), detail its manifestations, analyze its ecotransference resonances, note examples of its presence in the local community, go into detail about the reach of its shadow and traumatization, and suggest hostings that invite syndromes to soften back into motifs. The result of all the research should be an enhanced, describable deep dialog between the researcher and the place (myth, motif, neighborhood, hillside, etc.).

Quantified data should receive a *terrapsychologizing*[9] analysis to see whether the forces and outlines of placefield motifs recur as images and shapes in the numbers and grids. The original documentation that included fieldwork in Escondido, California, home of a powerful "devil's corner" motif, came unexpectedly to 666 pages. Such recurrences make the *genius loci* a co-participant not only in the assessment, but in evaluating the data.

Sharing the Findings

How the findings are presented depends on the setting in which they are used. In an academic setting, they might take the form of a thesis or dissertation, whereas for a journal, the organization of material will depend in part on the submission guidelines. An oral defense or presentation might require the use of images or sounds. The crucial consideration to bear in mind is that the presenter is speaking, in effect, on behalf of the place that was studied. The goal should be to make its animated presence as real as possible to the audience. Presentations that include interested members of the community enable them to participate in placehosting as well.

Closing the Study

A final ritual making creative use of an image or theme arising from the research site and, ideally, performed there brings the study to a close and expresses the researcher's gratitude as a final gift and bow to the *genius loci*.

———————

Thus Terrapsychological Inquiry, our proposed set of procedures for consciously inviting the spirit or soul of place to raise visible ripples in the waters of the human interior. In the following section, we will draw on some of these ideas to find our way deeper into myth, matter, and meteorology on our way back into an animated cosmos.

Terra Cognita: Homing in on the Within of Things

One afternoon an old Kiowa woman talked to me, telling me of the place in Oklahoma in which she had lived for a hundred years. It was the place in which my grandparents, too, lived; and it is the place where I was born. And she told of a time even further back, when the Kiowas came down from the north and centered their culture in the red earth of the southern plains. She told wonderful stories, and as I listened, I began to feel more and more sure that her voice proceeded from the land itself.

—N. Scott Momaday

CHAPTER SIX

Minding the Matter of Myth: Geography Archetypalized

> Those of us who live beneath this cold mountain
> have heard its voice in our dreams, felt its arms
> lift us out of warm rooms and soft beds, up
> onto its shoulders where we are light as leaves.
>
> —Amy Barratt, "The Mountain"

Upon entering the domain of classical Jungian interpretation, the specific images of places that appear in dream, art, fantasy, or ecotransference reactions are liable to be paired with a transpersonal, generalized archetype: Pacific Ocean as Collective Unconscious, Santa Barbara shoreline as Liminal Space or Threshold, this sturdy cedar as World Tree or Axis Mundi, that sparkling meadow as Pasture of Wandering Souls. For example, Jungian analyst Linda Schmidt describes her mother Jane Wheelwright Hollister's attachment to the Hollister Ranch where she grew up in California as evoking the presence of the Primordial Mother.[1] When such connections are made as a reflex or afterthought, the numinous features of these particular images of place are lost in the soothing folds of broad, archetypal constructs. This type of move, which subordinates an experience in all its particularity and detail to something larger than life, has been described as "archetypal reductionism."[2] When it happens to a feature of the terrain, terrapsychology refers to it as *psychification*: defending against the power of the tangible by covering it up with a universal.

Terrapsychology seeks to avoid this disconnection by honoring the specifics of place and the particular mythic figures that inhabit it. The psyche's natural language is mythological, a language of images and stories. *Myths matter because they are the collective dreams that wed inner and outer, people and places, known and unknown. Myths image deep structurings of the human experience of the nonhuman.* Because terrain unreduced to archetypes seems to speak this language too, a strange but powerful idea dawns that the imaginal presence of place is actually a kind of unconscious, a psychic layering of the world found right down in its texture and detail. As Jung noted, the gradual disenchantment of the world led to the symptomatic return of the exiled spirits of nature as psychic complexes and "inner" pain.[3] Industries and economies forged on the anvil of modernity depend on keeping the former sprites and dryads imprisoned within the human mind, for the alternative would be realizing that using up or damaging a "natural resource" is like depleting the artesian wellsprings of the psyche.

Nevertheless, certain mythic figures favor certain places. Every culture knows such place-favorings: Apollo's fondness for Delphi, YHWH's for hot-headed Sinai. Such pairings suggest important interdependencies between where we abide, Who inhabits the locale, and the tissue of mythic language that binds the two together. Terrapsychology examines these interdependencies in such a way that the imaginal and ecological details both remain in view. We cannot understand a place in detail without some sense of which folkloric figures gather there, whether angels in Los Angeles or innovative Prometheus in Switzerland. This area of study imagines geography as an abode of mythic presences.

ARCHETYPAL GEOGRAPHY

For James Hillman, mythic figures such as gods are not nouns, denoting objects or things; they are archetypal *beings,* "fundamental metaphors" or potentials of structure, "root ideas, psychic organs, figures of myth, typical styles of existence, or dominant fantasies that govern consciousness."[4] This moving from noun to verb is no verbal trick, but "a program of animism, of ensouling the nonhuman, a program that would relieve the human of its self-importance."[5] The question for such a program is not, "What pushes or pulls me?" as in what might be termed "Golem psychology," a psychology infiltrated by robotic push-pull fantasies. The question is, "Through which set of basic archetypal fantasies am I now gazing?" Does discovering some new hidden meadow evoke a Procrustean urge to reduce the experience to personal conflict? The Martian impulse to fight it down? The Vulcan need to fix it? The Aphroditic sensibility to appreciate its beauty? The Apollonian inspiration to poeticize it? From Whose altar do I encounter this new thing?

Archetypal geography extends this inquiry into which mythic presences and perspectives haunt a particular place. Hillman's call to recognize psyche's "polytheistic" fascination with pantheons of archetypes makes sense, for example, in terms of where he was when he uttered it: London, ancient site of numerous altars to numerous gods. London, where contemporary roadways follow their long-invisible Roman counterparts, where modern churches are unknowingly raised over ancient temples, where human works lie stratified in centuries of accumulated layers—and where Charles Darwin conceived a theory of evolutionary development in which later forms followed the outlines set by earlier ones. Whatever beings rove through London and its literal Underground, their polycentric love of historical layering seems to be infectious, adding a mythic dimension to ecological transference.

> At All Hallows, Barking, a buried undercroft and arch of a Christian church were constructed with Roman materials; a cross of sandstone was also found, with the inscription WERHERE of Saxon date; it is somehow strangely evocative of WE ARE HERE.[6]

Chapters 3-5 described how terrapsychology tracks the *genius loci*, the spirit or soul of a particular locale. Archetypal geography shifts the focus from the *genius loci* to the mythic presences attracted by the locale, as when "Escondida," the hidden river of imaginal vitality in Escondido, draws a Pan-like devilry into her vicinity. Key questions asked by this focus of study include: Who, mythically or folklorically speaking, inhabits this place? How do such inhabitants manifest ecologically, historically, and psychologically? How do they act when consciously recognized, and what happens when their presences go unregarded by the people who live there?

Consider the impressive figure of the Titan Prometheus, who disobeyed Zeus by giving the gift of fire (among other things) to humans—creatures that he himself had originally fashioned from clay and animated. Zeus, the All-father of the Olympian pantheon, was convinced that attempts to improve the lot of humans, huddling cold and naked down on Earth, would only increase their misery. So he forbade his fellow immortals from helping humankind. Prometheus disagreed with Zeus and, in an act of defiance, shared with humans the gifts of crafts, numbers, letters, medicine, the arts, the sciences, and the power to mine and reshape metals. He then scaled Olympus, stole fire from the chariot that pulled the sun across the sky every day, and gave the gift of fire to mortals too. A day soon came when the gods looked down from Olympus and beheld a race of fire-warmed artisans relishing their newfound independence.

When Zeus saw what was going on, he became so angry that Prometheus decided to offer him a specially cooked meal to calm him down. For this, Prometheus sacrificed a huge bull. But when the gods sat down to eat, they found no meat among the bones and gristle cleverly arranged on their plates. Prometheus had kept the best parts for himself and his human creations.

To pay Prometheus back for his defiance, Zeus ordered Hephaestos, the smith of the gods, to create Pandora, mother of women, as a gift-bearing bride for Prometheus. Her "gift"—the famous box or jar—contained perils and evils, which, if released, would devastate the human race. But Prometheus was suspicious of Pandora and her box, so he gave her to his brother, Epimetheus. His first plan for punishment having failed, Zeus now ordered Prometheus chained to Mount Caucasus. Every day the eagle Ethon came to pick at Prometheus's liver; every night his liver regenerated. Thus it went for generations, until Heracles came along, killed the eagle, and released the chastened Titan.

The name Prometheus, which means "forethought," suggests the qualities of existence he exemplifies: resistance to authority, suffering for insight, technological creativity, and the coaxing of life from lifelessness. His shadow side reflects brashness and hubris.

These Promethean themes have long characterized the mountainous geography of Switzerland. One of the most obvious is the resistance to authority. The nation's earliest recorded military revolts involved the Celtic Helvetian tribe resisting the Romans in 107 B.C.E. at the St. Bernard Pass. The Romans came on anyway, but were driven out again by the Altemanni. And so it went, with no one able to subject the country to centralized control for long, not even the Holy Roman Emperor or the powerful Hapsburgs. A wave of religious revolts two centuries later spread shockwaves all over the world, when Ulrich Zwingli and John Calvin and others of their ilk entered the craggy country. The long list of intellectual revolts in Switzerland includes names such as Jean-Jacques Rousseau of Geneva, temporary Swiss resident François-Marie Arouete (better known as Voltaire), whose anti-religious plays were banned, transplanted counterculture novelist Hermann Hesse, and the philosopher Friedrich Nietzsche, who lit bonfires up in the Engadine while building himself an Overman out of defiant fantasy.

Like Prometheus, alchemy concerned itself greatly with reanimating supposedly dead matter. One of alchemy's most famous practitioners, the physician Paracelsus, lived and worked in Basel, where, much later, Jung attended school. In Geneva, Mary Shelley wrote *Frankenstein*, "The Modern Prometheus," as her husband worked on *Prometheus Unbound*. They had been talking to Lord Byron about the possibility of animating dead flesh. Both worked in sight of where a future laboratory (CERN) would take matter apart one particle at a time and reassemble it.[7] Goethe, author of an early poem "Prometheus," as well as of the later masterpiece *Faust* (whose alchemist protagonist has often been compared to Prometheus), was repeatedly drawn to this mountain realm, where he spent several months on three separate occasions during his many travels. It was in a Bern Patent Office that the irreverent German-born naturalized-Swiss-citizen Einstein teased out the formula that would one day steal atomic fire from the very heart of matter and make it available for human use. In 1998, just south of the Alps, a European Union project named Prometheus conducted a fire experiment to study the propagation of forest fires. Without knowing it, all these innovative souls were working various aspects of the Prometheus myth, walking the countryside like Frankenstein's tall creation, a monster assembled with Promethean patience, but far more dangerous than any windup toy, anniversary clock, or Swiss Army knife.

No minor Promethean himself, Jung fashioned Complex Psychology[8] in Switzerland. His theory of types had been influenced by Swiss poet Carl Spitteler, Nobel Prize-winning author of *Prometheus and Epimetheus*. In *Psychological Types* Jung describes Spitteler's version of Prometheus as introverted and unconventional, and his counterpart Epimetheus ("Hindsight") as extraverted and conventional.[9] Of the dozen or so other references to Prometheus in Jung's *Collected Works*, one describes Faust's

"Godlikeness"[10] as Promethean in its quality of suffering for insight, and another speaks of the heroic freedom of the ego "chained to the Caucasus of the unconscious."[11] Jung views Faust, then, as a "medieval Prometheus."[12] Aware that the Romantics in particular tended to see Prometheus as a prototype of the daimon or natural genius, Jung clearly admired Prometheus's heroic willingness to make a supreme sacrifice to bring knowledge and power to mortals, but at the price of cutting himself off from the world—a consequence Jung would have viewed through the lens of a long tradition of Swiss isolationism.

The Introduction and other sections of this book have given examples of how the *history* and *ecology* of a particular terrain can reappear in the social and psychic life of its inhabitants, including their "inner" struggles, their relationships, and their dreams. Here we add the dimension of *myth*. For an archetypal geography, thematic connections join the mythic to the earthly, chronological, and human dimensions of a particular landscape. The following will imagine, examine, and speculate about how parallels between the figure of Prometheus and the history and geography of Switzerland came together in the life, work, and dreams of Jung. Through him we have a chance to discern the craggy forms of animated Helvetia *and* its resident progressive Titan, Prometheus.

JUNG IN PROMETHEAN HELVETIA

I ask the Earth, have not the mountains felt?
I ask yon Heaven, the all-beholding Sun,
Has it not seen? The Sea, in storm or calm,
Heaven's ever-changing shadow, spread below,
Have its deaf waves not heard my agony?

—Percy Shelley, *Prometheus Unbound*

Jung certainly picked an interesting place to be born in 1875.

The icy white heights of the Alps dominate more than half of this crossroads nation. The hundreds of lakes and thousands of pinnacles provide geographical extremes that even out below the Alps. Did those majestic, glacier-carved heights, twisted and shaped by patient tools of frost and crust, stand up tall in Shelley's imagination when he wrote about sad Prometheus, bringer of fire and the spark of life, chained so long to stony crests? Did they whisper to Nietzsche the idea of the superhuman Overman, or to Mary Shelley the tall, demonic form of the Frankenstein monster who pursued his creator across the icy slopes? Certainly one of these Swiss mountains, Monte Veritá in Ascona, served many seekers of truth—artists, philosophers, vegetarians, anarchists, dancers, contemplatives—from 1910 onwards as a kind of Caucasus hilltop hangout of innovative spiritual reform. Guests included anarchists Mikhail Bakunin and Peter Kropotkin; dancers Mary Wigman, Rudolf von Laban, and Isadora Duncan; writers Fanny von Reventlow, Erich Remarque, D. H. Lawrence, Franz Kafka, and Ernst Toller; artists Carl Eugen Keel, Paul Klee, and Ida Hofmann; spiritualist Rudolf Steiner; architect Henri van de Velde; social scientist Else von Richthofen; psychoanalyst (and anarchist) Otto Gross; and statesman Gustav Stresemann. Some of the visitors were in flight, as though having broken more than the rules of conventionality. Friedrich Glauser came to the mountain because he was running away from psychiatric incarceration; Hesse, from alcoholism; writer Hugo Ball and his wife, from the law. Jakob Flach came to animate puppets.

The Eranos conferences at Ascona, started by Olga Froebe-Kapteyn in 1933, provided more intellectual occasions to stop and think. "Eranos" signifies a banquet to which the guests bring their own food, and at which in the ancient Greek world wisdom and celebration were joined. Froebe-Kapteyn organized these festivals at the suggestion of religious scholar Rudolf Otto; for years the conferences were held at her estate, which served as a sort of Olympus for the day's leading innovative voices in spirituality (the first meeting discussed yoga and meditation), science, and, later, depth psychology. Jung was a frequent presenter at Eranos. Other presenters in cluded Martin Buber, Joseph Campbell, Karl Kerényi, Marie-Louise von Franz, Paul Tillich, Erwin Schrödinger, and Gershom Scholem. Sun screens gave the place an otherworldly glow: a fitting aura to what Henri Corbin described as a meeting open to the unforeseen, where speakers were expected to present from the edge, the very precipice, of their discipline.

Jung remained firmly within the Reformist tradition of his homeland. He hated conventionality as much as he hated church; his childhood dream of God shattering the glittering dome of the Basel Cathedral by shitting on it might have made even stern Calvin smile. For most of his life he felt quite alone, as Prometheus must have, in an ongoing engagement with God—

Prometheus exposed on a solitary rock, Jung concealed in the bowels of the earth. In his earliest recorded dream, he discovers a square hole in the ground near Laufen castle. Entering it and descending to ever deeper levels, he comes upon an erect penis standing on a golden throne. His mother's voice names the sky-watching object "the man-eater." (The Celts of the region had once indulged in cannibalism. Return of the ecohistorically repressed?) "Through this childhood dream I was initiated into the secrets of the earth. What happened then was a kind of burial in the earth, and many years were to pass before I came out again."[13]

Collecting fossils and minerals in the mountains near his home in Klein-Hüningen, dreaming of finding the bones of prehistoric animals in a burial mound by the river, equipping a secretly fashioned manikin with a black stone from the Rhine for use as a power source (as Prometheus had equipped his own new creations with fire)—all of these experiences convinced Jung that he must be on more intimate terms with the natural world, a world whose presence would stand behind so much of his work. Remembering the manikin in old age, for instance, he wrote: "… [T]here came to me, for the first time, the conviction that there are archaic psychic components which have entered the individual psyche without any direct line of tradition."[14] The manikin's stony source of Rhine energy recalls the importance Jung placed on the idea of psychic energy, which he connected to *mana* and its echo in the notion of a *genius loci*.[15] Earth, not Freud or Bleuler, served as Jung's first psychology instructor and informed his later theorizings.

Throughout his life, Jung was preoccupied with drowned corpses, and in fact he almost became one at a tender age when he tried to crawl through a guardrail at the Rhine Falls. As a boy, he saw a churchgoer drowned in the River Wiese, apparently right after the service. Later, as a man, Jung once mentioned to Freud his interest in a recent news story about corpses being found preserved in a peat bog. (Freud, incidentally, interpreted this fascination of Jung's with dead bodies to be indicative that the ambitious young Jung harbored a secret wish that Freud would die.) On another occasion, Jung found the remains of a French soldier beneath the stone tower he built at Bollingen. The man had drowned in the Linth in 1799, when the Austrians blew up the Grynau bridge. Corpses and cannibals out of the local past: Was Jung picking up on the dead and drowned Celts, soldiers, and Crusaders still floating in the imaginal memory of Switzerland, a land of frequent battles, resistances, revolts, and invasions? Did Bollingen summon him to put one more of the country's corpses to final rest? As a child, Jung had often drawn pictures of battles, played with fire, assembled fortified castles out of small stones. Was he re-enacting scenes out of the war-torn past of his fiercely protected home ground?

SHAPING THE STONE OF A TRANS-HUMAN PSYCHOLOGY

Recalling the manikin and its river stone prompted Jung, later in his life, to wonder about the possibility of a more-than-personal aspect to psyche; dreaming of a two-story house with medieval furnishings and Roman-era walls solidified this wonder into a hypothesis. In the dream, Jung lifts a stone slab and descends a staircase into the depths of a rocky cave containing scattered bones, broken pottery, and two half-disintegrated human skulls. The dream did more than revive Jung's interest in archeology.

> It obviously pointed to the foundations of cultural history—a history of successive layers of consciousness. My dream thus constituted a kind of structural diagram of the human psyche; it postulated something of an altogether *impersonal* nature underlying that psyche. … It was my first inkling of a collective a priori beneath the personal psyche. This I first took to be the traces of earlier modes of functioning. Later, with increasing experience and on the basis of more reliable knowledge, I recognized them as forms of instinct, that is, as archetypes.[16]

Note the geological texture of his terms: foundations, layers, structural, impersonal, nature, underlying, earlier—and this from a psychiatrist who regarded dreams as *natural* processes. Hints of an archetypal psyche, then, but buried in glaciated ground covered over by many thick strata of human history.

Most of the imagery pouring up out of Jung's famous "confrontation with the unconscious" after his break with Freud in 1913 cleaved closely to the natural world. Images of running water mixed with those of upwelling blood. He saw flames, scarabs, clouds, wheeling suns, and the mountains of Switzerland rising skyward to hold off floodwaters filled with corpses, a catastrophe envisioned not long before World War II. Jung's protective attitude toward his homeland seemed to match its protective attitude toward its inhabitants.

During this time, a figure called Philemon appeared often in Jung's fantasies and dreams. (In Greek mythology, Baucis and Philemon were an old Phyrgian couple visited by Zeus and Hermes shortly before the hard-hearted and inhospitable town where the couple lived was destroyed. In Goethe's telling of the Faust story, the couple stands in the way of Faust's ambitious project to reclaim some land from the sea.) An old male figure wearing kingfisher wings, Philemon tells Jung: Your thoughts are not products of the conscious mind. In their aliveness and autonomy they are more like animals in the forest, or people in the room, or birds in the air. Just after this rather ecological explanation, Jung saw a dead kingfisher washed up near a lake—yet another corpse found beside flowing Swiss water—not realizing, at least at first, how powerfully a land far older than he could imagine was signaling his attention with animals for words and dreams for speech. Philemon would countenance no easy psychifications.

In a dream that came to Jung shortly before his Promethean falling-out with Zeus-like Freud, an elderly Austrian customs official on the Swiss-Austrian border walks by Jung, stooping, with a peevish air of melancholic vexation. Someone in the dream says he is the ghost of a customs official who had died several years earlier. Jung connected the customs official with Freud and the customs check with analysis, but he did not pick up on the ecohistorically laden fact that Zürich had been founded as a Roman customs post.

In yet another dream, Jung realizes he has to kill "Siegfried." He associated the Siegfried of the dream with Wagner's famous hero and with Freud, whom he would later attack, with the ire of a disenchanted son, through decades of innovative writings. However, perhaps a local historical echo is found in this dream as well. Lurking behind the Siegfried dream figure is the Bohemian emperor Sigismund (this was also Freud's true first name), who in 1415 supported the Swiss reconquest of Hapsburg Aargau. Sigismund offered reformer John Huss safe passage to appear before the church leaders at the Council of Constance (1414) to defend himself against charges of heresy; but when the Council found Huss guilty of heresy, Sigismund withdrew his protection and Huss was arrested and burned at the stake. Jung could relate to Huss's sense of betrayal without suspecting that he himself was symbolically reliving it when Freud took him into his inner circle, only to cast him out when his newly developing theories no longer dovetailed with Freud's own.

The land continued to force its history back to life in Jung's dreams, fantasies, and synchronistic encounters, like a patient yearning to talk about a troubled past. Who better to address than the earthiest analyst in the country? In another dream, Jung found himself in an Italian village resembling the Kohlenberg in Basel. It is sometime between noon and 1:00 P.M., the hour of maximum illumination, and indeed the sun is out and very bright. To Jung's surprise, a knight in armor and wearing a white tunic with a red cross on it ascends some steps in full view of uninterested passers-by. None of the imaginal figures present share Jung's astonishment at this spectacle. Upon awakening from the dream, Jung linked the knight he had seen to the twelfth century.[17] The twelfth century held a special charm for Jung because he considered it the golden age of the science-art of alchemy. Paracelsus, one of alchemy's leading practitioners, had been born a few centuries later in Basel, where Jung went to school. (One of Jung's earliest fantasies was of making gold from magical copper roots.) The kingfisher image described above suggests the Fisher King from Grail lore, also dating back to the twelfth century, when monastic and Crusader activity peaked in Romanesque Switzerland. One post-Crusade day, Henry Dunant would swap the colors of the white Swiss cross and its red background and found the Red Cross Society in Geneva.

Persistent as underground history, persistent as place itself, the local Swiss themes of twelve, alchemy, corpses, and knights would not leave Jung alone. In another of his dreams, a white dove is transformed into a little girl. She tells him that she can shapeshift, but only when the male dove (Jung) is busy with the twelve dead. If the dove girl is a personification of the spirit of Basel (the "Basel Dove" has long been a prominent local image), she seems to be saying that she (Basel) can undergo transformation only to the extent that Jung busies himself with the Swiss past—the twelfth-century past in particular—buried but seething below him.

Jung's most ecopsychologically telling dream is the one in which he finds himself in a place similar to Alyscamps near Arles, where there is a lane lined with sarcophagi dating back to the distant Merovingian days. Seeing a similar line of tombs in his dream, the sleeping Jung is reminded of old church burial vaults topped with knights in armor. He takes a closer look. The first dead man in the row hails from the 1830s; he wakes under Jung's gaze. The second is from 1800, and he too comes to life. The rest, who are similarly revivified, date back to successively earlier times down to the last entombed figure, a twelfth-century crusader in chain mail. Jung feels sure that this last dead man at least is well and truly dead, but after a pause he comes back to life too. Even in dreams, the warmth of conscious attention can reanimate the undead local past.

Jung interpreted these historically weighty images as psychological symbols, but they continued to recur, perhaps because he did not consistently link them to the still-living "memory" of his ecoreactive homeland. To the extent that he did, their thematics softened from acted-out conflicts into Sermons to the Dead and painted stone walls. Nor could he see the extent to which the Swiss Crusader—the ecotransference of an unconscious identification with the land's historical themes—animated his lifelong attempt to rejuvenate Christianity psychologically, a task so many earlier Reformers had tried—unsuccessfully—to accomplish, because they lacked the Jungian tools of metaphor and myth. As Jung struggled to reinterpret dogmatized, literalized Christian images and rituals as deep psychological processes, *he* became the red-crossed knight from out of the reactive Swiss past. As he put it shortly before the onset of his "breakdown," "One fantasy kept recurring: there was something dead present, but it was also still alive."[18]

It has been speculated that Jung's confrontation with the unconscious, which began after his friendship with Freud ended, amounted to a psychotic break. If so, Jung was a very functional psychotic. Through four hard years he maintained a busy schedule of lecturing, writing, doing research, and seeing patients, while conducting an extensive self-analysis. Be that as it may, his confrontation repeats the Promethean/Swiss theme of spending time in a mountaintop purgatory while Philemon, the kingfisher-winged spirit, mentored him at night in his dreams.[19]

What finally relieved the weight of the inner pressure on Jung during this time was the act of hewing stone for the building of his tower at Bollingen. He decided to erect the tower when a boyhood memory surfaced: that of fashioning miniature castles from stones. He set aside a specific time—high noon—to construct fortified villages near his Kusnacht home on Lake Zürich. Placing a red rock as an altar stone for a tiny church, he was reminded of the phallus dream of his childhood. The best of his later ideas, he told secretary-biographer Aniela Jaffé, occurred to him while working at masonry, literally in touch with earthly sources of power, pressure, and history, sources that mentored his work to the degree that he remained open to their influence.

Yet still the corpses stalked him; hence his *Septem Sermones*, his spontaneous rendering of the *Seven Sermons to the Dead* who troubled him. He drew his first mandala after writing this funereal piece. The idea for the mandala came to Jung after he discovered the symmetrical *yantra* diagrams favored by meditating Tibetan Buddhists. Most mandalas are circular or four-sided, and are organized around a center. Jung interpreted them as spontaneous symbols of psychic wholeness. He drew them for years, before a pivotal dream brought a key phase of his inner confrontations to a close. In the dream, he finds himself in a "Liverpool" that resembles Basel near the Totengasschen, the "Alley of the Dead." Before him, atop a plateau, sits a broad square, where the streets of the city's quarters converge. Here he sees a pool with an island at its center and a tree upon the island. Jung overhears someone in the dream remarking that he can't imagine why a certain Swiss would want to settle here in Liverpool, but Jung, his eyes filled with the beauty of the living, numinous tree, thinks: I know why. With this dream, Jung believed, the goal had been revealed, for one cannot pass beyond the center. He wrote: "Through this dream I understood that the self is the principle and archetype of orientation and meaning."[20] He used "self" to mean the Self, the ultimate, archetypal symbol of totality, an entity he also referred to as the God-image.

On another level, this dream might disclose mandala-shaped Basel's perception of itself as a center or pooling of vital life. Naming itself Liverpool, a pooling of so much Promethean talent and liver-like regeneration, and displaying the imaginal beauty of its inner being, the Basel of Jung's dream seems to have held Jung's image gracefully within its own by dreaming about *him* as a solitary tree—a solitary truth ("truth" and "tree" share etymological roots)—planted in the center of an island. His relationship to that place was not one of ownership, but of belonging, of experiencing himself as a part of its wholeness. (A favorite tree he often sat under at his home was struck by lightning when he died.)

After this dream, the inner pressure eased, as though the mandalic city, the undead past, and the moist ground on which Jung plodded on bare feet had finally asked all they could of him in depicting his relationship to them in dream images. It is little wonder that he compared the lifelong flow of preoccupying images to an immense outpouring of lava, from which he shaped the crystal of his vocation.

But early in 1944, some other place summoned his attention, and the outcome felt like a gift. After breaking his foot(!) and suffering a heart attack, Jung hung between life and death in a vision of the Earth seen from the Olympian perspective of orbit. It moved him so deeply that he retained the sense of awe to his dying days. It was, he stated, the most glorious thing he had ever seen.

> At times I feel as if I am spread out over the landscape and inside things, and am myself living in every tree, in the plashing of the waves, in the clouds and the animals that come and go, in the procession of the seasons.[21]

When Jung's body entered the earth in 1961, he left behind a last recorded dream of alchemical gold gleaming from the roots of a square mandala of trees. It shone like sparks of the World Soul intertwined with his work in the living depths.

Haunted all his life by corpses, crosses, and the Promethean shadow of Switzerland, Jung not only crafted an opus that gave these images faithful psychic representation, but he left behind a body of work whose ecopsychological potential has yet to be adequately explored. Jung's closeness to the earth assured the reach and fidelity of this work where other, less grounded thinkers would have succumbed to blind actings-out devoid of later value except as examples of unmanaged ecotransference. Rather than being reducible to the surround, the psyche-nature connections of Jung's work illuminate the surround like sunlight and shadow seen through stained glass. These connections do not spark only in Switzerland, but bring the potential of new energy and Promethean fire to bear on our deep relations with places everywhere.

In Jung himself, Prometheus-Faust, mountainous Switzerland, the spirit of reform, and the spirit of the age melded together into a new amalgam—Complex Psychology—without bursting the alembic of his soul; and in this he was, as he often recommended that others try to be, a sturdy vessel of divine conflict.

Jung's life and work in Switzerland also underline the key premise of an archetypal geography: that inviting the local myths in tends an aspect of the imaginal ecology, just as keeping a friendly eye on the local soils tends the physical ecology. To the degree that we make space for the stories that dwell in particular places, we enrich our relations with the animated world, enlarge our understanding of ecocommunity as human, terrestrial, *and* archetypal, and learn something of where our own stories fit into larger patterns of earthly myths dreamed and framed by the land.

———————————

In Mary Shelley's tale, the Promethean alchemist took the stage as unwitting destroyer: "You seek for knowledge and wisdom, as I once did; and I ardently hope that the gratification of your wishes may not be a serpent to sting you, as mine has been."[22] In Percy Shelley's drama, Prometheus is presented as a noble redeemer who would "fain be what it is my destiny to be, the savior and strength of suffering man, or sink into the original gulf of things."[23] For Jung, the alchemists foreshadowed the insights of depth psychology by projecting unconscious images into matter while bent, deep in fantasy, over the bubbling and hissing alembics. But what if the alchemists were not projecting?

The alchemists thought that the opus demanded not only laboratory work, the reading of books, meditation, and patience, but also love.

—C. G. Jung

CHAPTER SEVEN

Chymical Subjectivity: Dialogical Alchemy

Remembering speechlessly we seek the great forgotten language, the lost lane-end into heaven, a stone, a leaf, an unfound door. Where? When?

—Thomas Wolfe, *Look Homeward Angel*

For two millennia, alchemists, the forerunners of chemists and research scientists, labored, experimented, and meditated in their laboratories in their quest for an "alkahest," "panacea," or "Philosopher's Stone" that could bestow long life and transmute common metals such as lead and iron into silver or gold. Alchemical studies intensified during the Middle Ages, as though taking up a counterposition to the religious preoccupation of Christians with otherworldly affairs. Those for whom the rituals and symbols of Christianity had lost their power to enchant or inspire sought wisdom in the depths of matter. During the Renaissance, some alchemists began to speculate openly about the Sacred Science's overtly spiritual possibilities. Perhaps inner and outer transformation went hand in hand. From this time forward, references in alchemy to chemical operations as metaphysical metaphors multiply.

Later, as the fields of chemistry and physics shrugged off the last vestiges of the metaphysical magic of alchemy, the texts left by the alchemists collected cobwebs in esoteric libraries—until Jung and his researchers began eagerly to gather them up.

JUNG AND ALCHEMY

Jung had recurring dreams about an annex library containing esoteric books bound in pigskin and engraved with copper symbols, but he did not recognize them as being about alchemy until 1926, when Richard Wilhelm sent him a copy of the *The Secret of the Golden Flower*, an ancient Chinese alchemical text. Jung promptly ordered books on alchemy, and he realized immediately that the alchemists were speaking a language he understood: that of psychological symbolism. On the surface, the alchemists were writing about the transformation of chemicals and minerals; but unconsciously, Jung concluded, they were describing images of psychological transformation. The angels, spirits, hermaphrodites, and monsters believed by alchemical researchers to inhabit their simmering chemical mixtures were really archetypal images projected from their psyches into matter: helpful guides, shadowy blockages, resplendent images of wholeness. Working in alchemy with material substances, then, in Jung's view, was an inadvertent way to work on one's internal evolution.

The alchemists themselves, however, did not view what they did in this way. They saw their task as much larger than that. It was the *world* they sought to rejuvenate, not primarily themselves.[1] Promethean Einstein once said he did physics to know God's thoughts; the alchemists wanted to know Terra's. They were interested in what matter was thinking about.

While Jung understood that, his writings about it are inconsistent. Sometimes he speaks of matter itself as animated, but at other times he insists that its animation derives from human projection—as when the alchemists saw inhuman forms in their concoctions. In this latter view, the world remains a human place after all because the shadowy evidences of aliveness in matter derive from projections of the human mind, not from the matter itself.

Jung's theoretical surmise that alchemists projected psyche into matter stood squarely on a concept coined by French anthropologist Lucien Levy-Bruhl. "The representation of the 'alchemystical' process by persons needs a little explanation. The personification of lifeless things is a remnant of primitive and archaic psychology. It is caused by unconscious identity, or what Levy-Bruhl called *participation mystique*. The unconscious identity, in turn, is caused by the projection of unconscious contents into an object …."[2] What Levy-Bruhl named *participation mystique* denotes the inability of "primitives" or of primitive states of consciousness to stand back from what they experience. Levy-Bruhl first published this eurocentric opinion in 1910 in his book *How Natives Think*. Without the benefit of any dedicated fieldwork experience, Levy-Bruhl articulated in scientific language the prevalent racist belief that aboriginal peoples think only prelogically—childishly, in fact, so childishly that they cannot tell their religious feelings apart from their objects of devotion. This is why they think everything is sacred.

Eventually, however, a barrage of criticism combined with exposure to data culled from real fieldwork convinced bedraggled Levy-Bruhl to abandon his model of the primitive mentality. In old age, he valiantly owned up to some of its more unhelpful cultural biases. Nevertheless, the earlier pages of Jung's *Collected Works* contain references to primitives, savages, childlikeness, superstitions, mental epidemics, *representations collectives* (another Levy-Bruhl concept), and the "animistic" delusions of people with "undifferentiated" minds. This bias carried over to his view of what went on between the alchemist and the materials he sought to transform.

Although the assumption that projection worked in alchemy as it does in therapy has come under criticism,[3] terrapsychology wonders what it would it mean to our understanding of psyche if the imaginal figures that swam into the alchemists' reveries over boiling, steaming, hardening, and melting ingredients were living images not projected after all. If the alchemists weren't projecting, if the things we manipulate bear their own qualities of psychic reality, as Jung believed[4] now and again, then the capacity for entertaining "animism" is not a symptom of primitivism, but a quality of active engagement with things. An unconscious identification with nature is not characteristic of primal cultures, therefore, but of dissociative civilizations estranged from the natural world and therefore living out an unconscious identification with it. "*Participation mystique*" needs redefining as a *heightened* participatory consciousness, and proceeds to the issue of what the alchemists really felt into during their transformative laboratory forays.

Terrapsychology offers the view that the alchemists were listening into, digesting, and writing down *what their ensouled materials precipitated into the alchemical imagination:* the alchemists were hearing the psychic sound of an animated world, with the substances they sought to transform serving as psychological portals into the world's interiority.

A Phenomenology of the Metals

It is no accident that alchemically-minded Goethe, the Faust tale's most famous reteller, found that if he tended to a plant, a moving image formed in his imagination, not as a generalization from the details his eyes took in, but as an experiential outgrowth of them. This movement-image he named the *Ur-plant:* a flow of living becoming similar to what Aristotle thought of as the Form or potential or essence of a thing, its innermost tendency to actualize its being. In the eye of *anschuung,* or "exact sensorial imagination," the depth that revealed itself lived not below or behind leaf and stem and blossom, but within them, just as the "meaning" or richness of a sonata floats *through* the music rather than hiding somewhere behind the composition.[5]

Chemistry looked at soils and compounds from the outside, but the alchemical "philosophic adepts" engaged fantasy, focus, piety, and love of probing the essence of matter's *withinness* and intuiting the structures of its subjectivity: a phenomenology of the metals. Seen interanimistically, *alchemy* (*al-kimiya:* possibly from "what is poured out," "sap," "juice," or "land of black earth") has handed down fabulously rich diagrams of what things look like to themselves when tended through powerful summonings of alchemical imagination. Those swampy demons and aerial angels may be clothed in European imagery, but at bottom they echo forth powerfully what mindful matter makes of its own interiority as reflected in the researcher's consciousness.

What would eventually emerge as key aspects of Complex Psychology made sense to Jung only *after* his chymical researches, so much so that he explicitly traced the roots of his concepts down into the alchemical depths.

> When I pored over these old texts everything fell into place: the fantasy-images, the empirical material I had gathered in my practice, and the conclusions I had drawn from it. I now began to understand

what these psychic contents meant when seen in historical perspective. My understanding of their typical character, which had already begun with my investigation of myths, was deepened. The primordial images and the nature of the archetype took a central place in my researches ....[6]

A few pages later he adds that alchemy provided the ground for his confrontations with the unconscious. He came to see this rite of passage as a sustained experiment in alchemical transformation.

The implications of Jung's statements about this are enormous. Not only did poring over the procedures reveal to him a wider and earthier appreciation of the archetypes (for he was right after all to link them, albeit half-knowingly, to a native sense of participatory sensitivity), it gave him a framework *and* a language for understanding "inner" experience. Primordial patterns, mythic structures, movements in the unconscious, psychological transformation: freed from the fetters of outmoded anthropology, these deep currents meander beyond exclusively human concerns to circulate through the heart of the matter from which all concerns ultimately spring and to which they eventually return. It could take ages to grasp even the basics of the eco-imaginal legacy left by the alchemists.

Reimagining this sacred science puts the substance back into it. A brief revisioning of the alchemical opus from its initial labors to its legendary completion reveals a much earthier intersubjective project than either infusing spirit into matter or withdrawing from the earthly into more psychified realms of being.

THE OPUS REANIMATED

It has often been claimed that the alchemists took over from Aristotle and pre-Socratic philosophy the idea that everything is formed out of one primal substance, invisible to the eye but visible to the mind. The ancient Greeks called this principle the *arche*, and many held the gods to be symbols or expressions of it. In fact, as Marie-Louise von Franz points out, "A great part of what we recognize today as being psychic belonged, in the view of the old Greeks, to a superindividual, objective world soul."[7] The alchemists called it Mercurius and equated it with *anima mundi*.[8]

In alchemical theory, this primal god-stuff or soul-stuff made everything grow, even minerals buried in the earth. These minerals ripened very slowly as they evolved from "base" metals, such as lead, into "noble" ones such as gold. In fact, the truest kind of gold was said to be of a greenish color like that of a plant. This "non-ordinary" gold represented a particularly pure distillation of the greening force of the primary substance. The adept's job was to assist the evolution of the metals into purer, "greener," and livelier states. In terrapsychological terms, the alchemists aimed at giving more interactive consciousness to the World Soul whose sparks of aliveness invest everything with animation. Distilling the substances helped them become more congruent with their essential nature, in effect less reactive and perhaps more "aware" of their substantiality by "seeing" themselves mirrored in deep human reflection. The alchemical *vas* (vessel) makes an appropriate symbol for the psychological field in which things demonstrate their qualities of corporeal mindfulness.

To do this, the alchemists started with what Aristotle had called "*prima materia*" (prime matter), a material sample of soul-stuff. No one knows for certain what the alchemists meant by *prima materia*. Its synonyms are legion—dirt, urine, feces, quicksilver, ore, iron, lead, salt, sulphur, vinegar, water, air, fire, earth, blood, cloud, sky, dew, shadow, sea, moon, raw chaos— but most agreed that the *prima materia* did not sit on thrones or mountaintops; instead, it was common, hidden everywhere, and "*in sterocore invenitur*" (found in filth). Jung interpreted *prima materia* psychologically as a point of interest or turbulence emerging from the unconscious when a conflict, an immaturity, an old wound called for attention and work. The profusion of natural symbols adorning descriptions of the *prima materia* and the numerous descriptions of it as "dead" also suggests the earthier, less human-centered idea that the prime matter is *any* ordinary substance whose qualities yet remain untinged, and therefore unawakened, by an appreciative witnessing in close proximity to it. The same broken door or cracked sidewalk or stand of stone passed by day after day is a silent partner left out of a potentially sensuous dialog. Prime matter: a happening waiting for an attention-triggering accident.

In terms of the Earth as a whole, *anima mundi* awaiting alchemical assistance is not "unredeemed" because stuck in crude materiality, but because so many hearts do not sense or hear or appreciate her—we whose qualities of mindfulness derive from *her* patient evolutionary alchemy. The roundness of the Rotundum, a final evolution of the Stone, hints at her presence,[9] however, and Mercurius, the spirit of that *lapis*, is repeatedly tied to her.

Many alchemists insisted that one must start with a bit of the Stone— a consciously observed spark of the World Soul—to produce more Stone. One begins the operation with an intuited sense of its animistic import: Nature summons forth the work. The growthful essences of everything material, says Helvetius, are hidden in their outward forms like the kernel hidden in the nut.[10] The *Splendor Solis* (1598), attributed to Salomon Trismosin, puts it succinctly: "This Stone of the Wise is achieved through the Way of Greening Nature."[11] The opus is therefore a kind of natural science amplified by the dimension of depth.

Placing the prime matter into an alembic, the alchemist used various procedures to break down the substance into its four elements (air, water, fire, earth), which in turn subsided into "Sol and Luna" or King and Queen, figures symbolizing the chemical opposites of gold and silver, or sulphur and salt, thought to bind matter together. These opposites were then reunited— cooked together—through a *coniunctio* (conjunction) or "chymical marriage" that replaced the four elements' original state or "Dragon" of undifferentiated chaos with a fifth element or "Phoenix" (rebirth self-imaged) in which all chemical forces and spirits achieved harmonious interrelations. In psychological language, exposing a point at issue with the light of consciousness frees it from repression, cleanses it of unhelpful biases and outworn attitudes, unearths the archetypal fantasies behind it, and allows its integration into the rest of the personality.

The quintessential product of all this was the marvelous Philosopher's Stone, which Jung took to be a symbol for the Self or God-image, blueprint of the ego and archetype of totality. Working from within a Christian framework of personal salvation, Jung believed the alchemical opus to be a work of redemption whose end result put the alchemist in touch with healing spiritual forces emanating from the unconscious, and not from reconstituted elements simmering in the *vas*. Psychological maturity in the Jungian view demanded a withdrawal of projections and unconscious identifications from external "hooks" such as chemicals and compounds.

If we shelve the projection hypothesis, however, inquiry turns instead toward the subjectivity *of things* in fermentational dialog with the alchemical imagination. The operations that break down the prime matter then seem more like attempts to analyze its psychic presence—or its sense of emplacement—prior to reorganizing the alchemists' perceptions of the materials into an adequate conceptual framework or sense of understanding. With their spirit or "inner power of the material"[12] now appreciated instead of being atomized or beaten into symbols, the elements take on an ennobled sheen, just as places listened into emanate a more harmonious presence. Each opens a doorway into the psychic heart of matter.

PHILOSOPHER'S STONE AS "VITALIZED MATTER"

Many an alchemist awoke to write down a dream of being directly addressed by some personified metal or other showing up at night as a guiding figure. Alchemy takes these spiritual forces to be inherent in matter rather than placed there by projection. According to Paracelsus, the gods are buried in the *prima materia*, to their undoing and ours.[13] Spirit, Jung suggested, is nearly always related in alchemy to water, and often hidden in it like a fish;[14] the recurrent theme of ascent and descent derives partly from water's evaporation into rain-bearing clouds.[15] When imaged as fire, spirit flares from the center of the earth. Famous gems mined from the depths contain fabulous powers; magical imps and goblins inhabiting folk tales dwell near certain mines and other earthly sites.[16]

> The attributes of the stone—incorruptibility, permanence, divinity, triunity, etc.—are so insistently emphasized that one cannot help taking it as the *deus absconditus* in matter. … What unconscious nature was ultimately aiming at when she produced the image of the lapis can be seen most clearly in the notion that it originated in matter and in man, that it was to be found everywhere, and that its fabrication lay at least potentially in man's reach.[17]

But the deity has not absconded. It was there all along, hidden in plain sight and ignored like the stone that the builders rejected, only to recognize it later as the cornerstone.

Has it spoken up loudly enough? Although alchemical images and descriptions do not attribute projection to the alchemist, they do attribute it to the materials; there is even a *proiectio* phase in the creation of the Stone. Its spirit penetrates everything, including imperfect metals, which an old manuscript compares to sleepers chained in Hades until awakened by the radiating Tincture.[18] "… It hath the virtue to communicate itself to vegetables and Animals, and to every inferior body to make them perfect …."[19] And like the radiant presence of place, it can poison as well as heal.

According to legend, the spiritually potent Stone not only cures, kills, or extends the span of life; it can also make more of itself (*multiplicatio*), either directly or by being passed through ever more rigorous refinements. This brings to mind Teilhard de Chardin's image of an evolving Earth compressing its "radial" (inner, psychic) energies into a concentrated field of "vitalized matter" and "Life squared."[20] In terms of things and places, it would seem that a sympathetic sensitivity to them somehow concentrates their essence and encourages its expression, just as a garden grows more richly when given loving attention. "Now, if this Salt and Sulphur are purified sufficiently, and the distilled spirit, or extracted tincture, added, Nature finds a subject wherein she can carry her operations to the highest limit, if an artist furnishes her with proper vessels, and a degree of heat suitable to her intentions."[21]

What, then, is the Philosopher's Stone? A Self symbol, as Jung thought? But what about the things themselves? Is it the meditation and "true imagination" indispensable for the opus? The alchemists envisioned something substantial, whether hard like rock, fine like powder, or flowing like a blessed tincture or "panacea" reunited with its own intangible potentials. They would have seen the severance of the material and the psychic as a failed *coniunctio*, a missed conjunction, and so, no doubt, would their materials.

Perhaps the ubiquitous Stone comes into being with any delving deeply and imaginatively into things, locales, conditions of existence, any bit of world or nature treated with conscious respect and empathy until its presence begins to glow and solidify in the imagination. The Stone could be any chunk of revivified prime matter, such as an arbor or street corner sparked into psychic self-expression in dreams or fantasies or "synchronistic" events by the chymical reconciliation of self and place.

The Stone's legendary transparency reflects the visibility of its vital "seed" or soul to the researcher who looks through it as through a lens and sees the imaginal workings of surrounding matter. It therefore heals the alchemist, whose tie to the world is remade, and heals "the metals" by replacing unconsciousness of them with awareness of their aliveness. The *Lapis Philosophorum* comes to life in every leaf, granule, strand of hair, or plot of land that allows re-entry into an enchanted, soulful world. It serves as a key to open a forgotten passageway out into some inspirited terrain, like the chunk of iron that led Teilhard de Chardin to God. It also points back at our own mysterious crevices, chemistries, unpolished surfaces, and mineralizations, as Matthew Cochran's "archetypal geology" says so poetically:

> The fact is we are born with these primary cracks, cleavages, our fault lines, our fractional crystalline structure, just like any stone, igneous, sedimentary or metamorphic, we are marked by strata, vesicles, textures (just look at our labyrinthine brains) and these portals and pathways lead into our deep cavernous interior, with unrecognized fossils, generations of petroglyphs, symbols of old, our clandestine chambers full of passionate magma, our ancient water pockets, veins mineralized by silver, tungsten, copper, or flakes of gold … these ways in allow erosion to carve and expose us causing our soul's secrets to stand out like cinder cones, monuments, mesas and cliff faces—landmarks for others to encounter. Somehow through weathering we become more visible. We are seen.[22]

Where its glow travels then is very mysterious. It bears remembering that Gerhard Dorn, who advised other alchemists to turn themselves into living Philosophical Stones, was the adept who believed the opus incomplete until the laborer and the Stone were rejoined with the world. He probably suspected that the true adepts were really the compounds, which perform their own projections and multiplications of what light we manage to bring them. The alchemists do insist that when enough "heat" is applied, the reaction continues on its own. These emanations, which reinforce each other as they spread, might also be looked upon as exchanges of deep, mutual nourishment (the Stone was often called "divine flesh") passed back and forth through an interactive field between natural forces and human psychodynamics, each enlivening the other.

At its best, then, alchemy not only envisioned possibilities for individuation, but enlarged them into a renewed sense of contact with the inward power of outwardly handled matter. It bridged not only Gnosticism and modernity, and conscious and unconscious, but by inviting the introverted initiate into a wider world of suprapersonal beings and living forms, it breached his solitude by wearing it down experiment by experiment.

Edinger[23] noted that alchemy's fascination with *coniunctio* produced chemistry and physics on the extraverted side and depth psychology on the introverted side. Terrapsychology seeks to hold them together while centering both in the presence of place. Unlike Faust, who had to enter another world to find redemption, the alchymical researcher eats the "divine food" of the Lapis by partaking of *anima mundi* one earthen detail, experiment, and encounter at a time. Each brightens the greenish gold of an interanimistic *coniunctio*, a shared sense of the World Soul's self-rejuvenating immortality.

> … [F]or it comforteth the healthy, strengtheneth the weak, and maketh the aged seem young, and driveth away all grief, and putteth venom from the heart; it moisteneth the arteries and joints; it dissolveth all things in the lungs; it cleanseth the blood; it purgeth the pipes, and keepeth them clean; and if the sickness be of one month's continuance, it healeth it in one day, if of one year's continuance, it healeth it in twelve days, and if the grief be very old, it healeth it in one month. To conclude, whosoever hath this medicine, he hath an incomparable medicine above all treasures of the world.[24]

Throughout my whole life, during every minute of it, the world has been gradually lighting up and blazing before my eyes until it has come to surround me, entirely lit up from within.

— Pierre Teilhard de Chardin

CHAPTER EIGHT

Terra's Psychology: Natural Disasters and Sacred Sites, Human Halves and Animated Wholes

> If human consciousness can be rejoined not only with the human body but with the body of earth, what seems incipient in the reunion is the recovery of meaning within existence that will infuse every kind of meeting between self and the universe, even in the most daily acts, with eros, a palpable love, that is also sacred.
>
> —Susan Griffin, *The Eros of Everyday Life*

Natural disasters and sacred sites would seem to epitomize extreme opposites, as would the technological colonizers who flew out of the bird-shaped Fertile Crescent and the rooted, lore-weaving peoples they probably believed they were leaving behind. But is it possible that discernible, pulsating metaphors redolent of the imagistic language of Terra might emanate from such polarizations like thumps of the terrestrial heart?

NATURAL DISASTERS (ACTS OF GAIA)

When Katrina collapsed the levees of New Orleans in 2005, religious fundamentalists argued that the hurricane carried God's punishment to the sinners infesting the notorious Big Easy.[1] Nonsense, retorted the scientific evolutionists. Katrina simply represented yet another mindless combination of winds, waters, and heat exchanges. Terrapsychology offers a third alternative by holding open the conjecture that unusually violent acts of nature are neither punitive nor random, vengeful nor meaningless. Rather, when seen through the eye of interanimistic metaphor, they conform to predictable patterns, one of which, as we have seen, is: *nature turns toward us the face that we collectively turn toward it.* It is as though our ever more destructive behavior toward Earth were rousing responses in kind: not only in mechanical accord with the systemics of the Gaia Principle, but with all the reactivity, brutality, and sheer unconsciousness of any force of nature pushed too far out of balance. From the outside, or manifest level (to use Freud's terminology), we record a moving vortex driven by planetary exchanges of steadily accumulating warmth; from the inside, or latent level, a cleansing, rotating, destructive parody of an oil drill spinning around an aptly named "eye." The difference in views is not one of explanation, but of imagination, reinterpretation, and depth. Terrapsychology's shorthand for this shift of perspectives to get at the experiential, symbolic truths within animistic thinking is *lorecasting.* Too often the lore contains tragic consequences that cannot be explained away.

Earthquakes

No one expected the Sumatra-Andaman earthquake and tsunami that killed more than 275,000 people throughout South-east Asia at the end of 2004, but in retrospect it seems to have been the first in a recent escalation of "natural" disasters that include mad cows, superstorms in the Gulf of Mexico, and an imminent avian flu pandemic. The epicenter lay approximately 160 kilometers (100 miles) off the coast of Sumatra in the Indian Ocean. Twenty miles down, where the India Plate slithers below the Burma Plate, a slippage 400 kilometers (about 250 miles) long unzipped with enough force to displace seven cubic miles of water and to cause a subtle shift in the planet's spin. As the sea bed rose, so climbed the global sea level, and the average height of the Earth's crust with it. Things came to the surface concretely as well as symbolically as the length of a day shortened slightly. Islands and coastlines shifted restlessly. The earthly fabric was still unraveling an unheard-of three hours after the first detonation. The series of seismic concussions rang the great globe like a warning gong sounded repeatedly in an emergency. It remains to be seen whether it also signaled the crossing of some ecologically crucial line.

Against all the odds, it struck nearly to the hour on the anniversary of the 2003 quake that destroyed the Iranian city Bam and the fortress watching over the Old Silk Road.

Nature turns toward us the face that we turn toward it. If so, what makes these quaking places similar, that they would manifest what looks like similar responses to a consciousness sensitized to symbolic modes of reality?

Both Sumatra and Bam were historical highways of finance, industry, and conquest. Bam is on the Old Silk Road that Alexander the Great and Marco Polo traveled; inventions such as gunpowder and the compass were carried along it to make possible an Age of Exploration that would feed the forges and blast furnaces of the Industrial Revolution. Ecologically speaking, Bam has been an accomplice to the colonially financed devastation of the ecosphere. But the Road ran both ways: its 1346 opening carried the Black Plague from Asia to Europe.[2]

Like Bam, Sumatra ("Isle of Gold"), a noted exporter of petroleum and precious metals—and lumber before its rainforests fell to the saws of unbridled logging, sits near an important trade route. In fact, the India-China sea passage is the watery equivalent of the Old Silk Road. But Sumatra's ecological significance is not confined to the past. The region holds what could be the world's largest reserves of natural gas. Oil is plentiful there too. Suits against the world's largest petroleum corporation were biding their time in court dockets in the capital city of Aceh, where Exxon marked the spot near the epicenter, when the ground from which so much had been taken and the sea over which so much industry-building wealth had passed finally began to shake things upward.

Bam, Sumatra, the timing, the locations: if Earth were animate, these eruptions would look like self-protective ragings striking out at the pathways of so much wounding.

Still more recently, somewhere between Bam and Sumatra, in disputed Kashmir, where "freedom fighters" bombed cars and Indian troopers fired back, Muslims celebrating Ramadan and Hindus celebrating Durga Puja on October 8, 2005 found themselves caught in the center of a mighty seismic palm.

The shaking that erupted 25 kilometers (16 miles) under the earth probably released only a tenth of the stored seismic energy,[3] yet it killed a hundred thousand people and left three million homeless in Pakistan. The parts of Kashmir controlled by India also suffered deaths, building collapses, and numerous landslides. Hundreds of students and soldiers died in structures left unmodified because money was allocated to "defense." Journalist Sandip Roy's observation invites somber thought:

> Pakistani newspapers describe the death toll in "Indian-held Kashmir." The Indian dailies talk about the devastation in "POK" or "Pakistan Occupied Kashmir." But looking at the pictures it's hard to tell from which side of the line of control they come. As Agha Shahid Ali wrote, "In the lake the arms of temples and mosques are locked in each other's reflections."[4]

Whether or not warring parties surmise anything from Kashmir or Sumatra about nature's reactivity to conquest and control, the trembling ground left an anguishingly ironic metaphor broken out between tectonic plates colliding below territory fought over and divided up for centuries. "As above, so below," quoth the alchemists, but the reverse seems equally true in unstable territories where unthinking authorities build artificial divisions over natural gaps, ruptures, and places of entry into the depths. "The quake that crushed thousands of lives," announced *The Telegraph* out of Calcutta, "has cracked open the Line of Control."[5]

Hurricanes

Before threatening Texas, where the oil well that changed history first blew at Spindeltop, Hurricane Katrina had spun like an angry top over layers of sediment rich with petroleum first put to industrial use by conquistador Hernando de Soto in 1540. The first offshore oil well (1934) was dug into the ground with a rotary drill a mile off the coast of Louisiana.[6]

At one time, before levees and canals diverted it, silt from the Mississippi River had formed a natural storm barrier on the coast, but with the draining of the wetlands to make space for urbanization, New Orleans began to sink into a self-made depression, probably deepened by depressurization caused by oil extraction. Katrina swept in unhindered over a million acres of submerged wetlands and small coastal islands eroded by oil and gas canals and headed for a city founded to facilitate the atmosphere-darkening oil exploitation and transportation sucking its surrounding wetlands dry of vitality. (A third of the nation's oil and a quarter of its natural gas pass through New Orleans.) Consider the progression: U.S. troops fighting for oil in one Gulf, then an enormous disturbance named Katrina barreling down on oil refineries in another Gulf, as though by way of an unconscious but uncannily meaningful response. In a dream, such an event would suggest an imaginal attempt to rebalance a destructive conscious attitude. Meanwhile, the depressed geological heart that is New Orleans is sinking, and its suffering inhabitants with it. Others might maintain a manic denial about the ship of state in a stormy world, but for them, the party is over.

Having crippled the Mexican tourism industry, Hurricane Wilma blew ashore near Cape Romano as the fourth major hurricane to make landfall in one season, an event never before recorded. As lethally uncaring as any monstrous piece of meteorology, the superstorm landed almost exactly where Ponce de León had stopped in 1513 to look for gold and slaves. It washed over this site as though resolved to obliterate his footprints. (Tropical diseases have tended to function as more proactive defenses against human incursion. They held off colonization of the New World and Africa and almost stopped the Panama Canal from being built.) Those in search of ecological metaphors swirling in the unblinking eyes of such stormy self-cleansings might consider the names selected "at random" to describe them, starting with Tammy, "Perfect One," and moving on to Katrina, "Pure," Rita, "Right," and Wilma, the most powerful Atlantic hurricane on record: "Determined Protector."

Animals

As for animals, they had an extended field day around the world in 2006. Conditioning them to protest or parody human incursions could not have been more startling than what some did. Rampaging elephants, neither starving nor mistreated, blocked roads and stampeded villages in Uganda. Some of their parents had been hunted many years before. A 14-foot crocodile mauled a chainsaw in Australia while leaving its operator unharmed. In the U.S., a pelican high on domoic acid flew through the window of a car in Laguna Beach. A deer ran into a woman's house in Ohio and stomped her badly enough to send *her* to the emergency room. Sea lions at Newport Beach boarded boats, wrecked their cabins, and almost sank a yacht. A TV personality accustomed to treating animals as stage props was speared through the heart by a manta ray hidden below the surface and died in agony unbearable to witness. As of 2006, 38 new pathogens had moved from animals into humans over the last 25 years alone.[7] Animals in dreams sometimes show up as messengers. The message, if there is one, seems clear, if brutally so: enough encroachment, sprawl, pollution, entertainment, and ecological hubris is enough. Back off!

Holding the actions of quakes, storms, animals, and the like as ecological metaphors foregrounded and amplified by centuries of destructive colonization, industrialization, and conquest prompts very different questions than keeping to purely causal-linear considerations that hold us entirely separate from (and unaccountable to) the terrain and its occupants, both of which then remain safely devoid of any symbolic or communicative significance. Is the wild nature spirit of long-denied Pan running loose in our border-defying, population-thinning pandemics? Or in *Pan troglodytes troglodytes*, the chimp species source of the virus that mutated into HIV once Africa lay open to hunters and tourists? Does it mean anything that coronaviruses wear halo-like crowns? Do birds carrying flu also serve as auguries, as they did in ancient Rome,[8] as they fly like feathered parodies outward along the trade routes of imperial expansion? Why are the cows really mad? What grueling questions the suspicion of a reactive planet forces us to ask! Little wonder that so many prefer their matter good and dead.

For those with a sense of its aliveness, however, a terrapsychological take points backward to a long—no, ancient—tradition of experiential validation of intuitive and imaginative knowings and forward from them onto new interactive ground. A "thought of the heart" by James Hillman is worth pondering here:

> The world, because of its breakdown, is entering a new moment of consciousness: by drawing attention to itself by means of its symptoms, it is becoming aware of itself as a psychic reality.[9]

A becoming that summons our own awareness of it as such, not only through the wounds, the deaths, and the lingering, anguishing tragedies it inflicts on us time and again, but through contact with its more welcoming faces.

Sacred Sites

> It is no mere coincidence that our feelings about a place take
> on spiritual dimensions. An old rancher once told me he thought
> the lines in his hand had come directly up from the earth, that
> the land had carved them there after so many years of work.
>
> — Gretel Ehrlich, "Landscape"

The pyramids at Giza: skyward heights over gloomy crypts. Cahokia: an immense mound of earth with winged figures and cross-shaped symbols painted on prehistoric artifacts found beneath it; one day the Trappists would build a monastery there.[10] Mount Fuji: itself a monastery rising high above the volcanic fires warming its sacred grottos. The Bighorn Medicine Wheel: a stony, sacred hub whose celestially aligned spokes almost seem to anticipate the sweeping beams of a nearby radar dome. Stonehenge: a Stone Age calendar tracking stars and seasons above depths where Merlin is fancied still buried in magical sleep.

The world over, sacred sites are places where the celestial and terrestrial thematically interpenetrate as earth gods and sky gods meet in greeting. Serving as the geographical equivalents of the spiritually grounded psyche, they are sites where earthly tokens of affection are exchanged between the human and divine, like the coins and trinkets once offered to Artemis in her city of Ephesus. Such places are loci of spiritual energies so powerful that tapping into them through symbols can lend outworn ideologies new vitality. As such they are generous givers, sometimes through self-sacrifice, of plentiful life-changing psychospiritual gifts.

Whether Giza or Glastonbury, Lourdes or Fuji, the Ganges or the Rock of Cashel, Teotihuacan or the Janus-possessed Great Mosque of Cordoba, *sacred sites thematically express beneficial conjunctions of high and low, the earthly and the heavenly*, like Ganga flowing earthward through the celestial hair of Shiva. They present landscapes described as ethereal and skyscapes of stellar geography, heights found in depths, peaks in vales, interiors all around. Founded over an underground temple, Teotihuacan is laid out so that it points at distant mountaintops. As far as the sites are concerned, even the upperworld, skyward, celestial figures so prominent in human divinations and upward-gazing devotions *are aspects of the landscape*, a landscape felt to be holy.

Like genuine saints, like mentors of the soul, not all sacred sites are publicly identifiable as such. From Belden Lane:

> The uncanny thing was that I had been invited to the place, I had felt the deer (I felt some presence) in the clearing a good ten or fifteen minutes *before* she came. … Having spent the day searching for mana, for mystic voices, a luminous encounter with the Other, I met simply a deer. Walking back home, toward the vanishing red sunset, with honking geese passing high overhead, I felt an enormous joy.[11]

From George Seferis:

> I know a pine tree that leans over near a sea. At mid-day it bestows upon the tired body a shade measured like our life, and in the evening the wind blowing through its needles begins a curious song as though of souls that made an end of death, just at the moment when they begin to become skin and lips again. Once I stayed awake all night under this tree. At dawn I was new, as though I had been freshly quarried.[12]

The word "invited" in Lane's account is important. Although worthy studies in their own context, ley lines, geomancy, *feng shui*, cursus, nature art, monuments, and shrines, or for that matter memorials to saints and soldiers, cannot *make* a site sacred by dint of reputation or deed. Instead, such sites, including those consecrated by precious human blood, call out to the human rememberer as *witnessed*. Lama Anagarika Govinda sensed this clearly:

> The great rhythm of nature pervades everything, and man is woven into it with mind and body. Even his imagination does not belong so much to the realm of the individual as to the soul of the landscape, in which the rhythm of the universe is condensed into a melody of irresistible charm. Imagination here becomes an adequate expression of reality on the plane of human consciousness ….[13]

More: it opens the human witness to the unmistakable sense of *being* witnessed. Describing their anthology *The Sacred Place: Witnessing the Holy in the Physical World*, W. Scott Olsen and Scott Cairns say about the authors and their work, "The tone here leaves open the question of whether one bears witness to *something seen* or to *something by which one sees*."[14] "By which one sees." This sounds very much like an archetypal style of consciousness, with perceptions framed by the spirit of place.

Those trained to think spirit otherworldly might shudder to learn that the Coptic letters of the name "Moses" mean "water" and "tree"; that Sinai is a province of the moon and its cow goddess; that El Khider is akin to the Green Man; or that Solomon was said to control winds and understand the language of birds. Palamedes drew inspiration for inventing the alphabet after watching flocks of migrating cranes against the sky.[15]

Given the power of the *genius loci* and the numinosity of sacred land, it is no wonder that religious systems use nature symbolism in order to borrow some of its spiritual strength. Biblical images of heaven resemble Eden, as Haviva Pedaya points out, in a mandalic four-foldedness associated with the four seasons, four cardinal points, the four letters of the Ineffable Name.[16] Sefiroth are symbolized by stars or branches, chakras by flower petals. The Rig Veda praises holy herbs more ancient than the gods themselves. Krishna compares his essence to that of the fig tree; trees in Haiti are thought to guard children born near them. "The leaves of the tree," so proclaims Revelation 22:2, "are for the healing of the nations."

When describing the function of symbols, Jung compared images invested with psychic intensity to dams and waterwheels harnessing natural energy. With the rise of urbanization and organized religion, the natural sources of spiritual power began to be dis*placed* by the social structures that relied upon them. Where villages had grown up around sacred sites, medieval cities soared around cultic centers in Northern Europe, where no city could be considered one without hosting a cathedral.[17] It is no accident that the word *civitas* was often used for "castle." Those in search of spiritual renewal had to make pilgrimage to the new sacral object of the bell-governed community. With fewer and fewer exceptions, simple grottoes, streams, mountains, and valleys were now deemed insufficiently holy. As cities shaped like mandalic symbols of wholeness aligned themselves with the cardinal directions or radiated outward from central points of authority, the landscape's ancient witnesses to acts of human piety found themselves seen as objects, their minerals and waters sold as amulets and trinkets. From the cardinal to the urban to the political and the religious, the flow of psychic energy and emphasis from occupied landscapes energized ever more ethereal projects.

According to the Gospel of Thomas, the Kingdom of Heaven is "spread out over the earth." Indeed. Strange to find after all that churches, processions, cults, sects, creeds, pledges, titles, badges of office, coinages, cities, counties, nation-states, and unsustainable civilizations survive by taking on, in symbolic garb, the features of sacred terrain, and by doing so divert the power of place.

Unless reconnected at last to their root sources, however, these diversions never endure. Clocks might borrow the rhythms of nature, and messianic missions remove the holy here to the end of linear time, but entire societies run down and expire once severed from respectful contact with the globe that feeds them. "If place can be fenced in," Lynda Sexson adds, "then the sacred will mock the fence from outside the boundary."[18]

Naturally. The archetypal Trickster is a force of nature too, and unnatural divisions between people and places sell out bright possibilities to a dissociated past. For those who revere sites brimming with spiritual power, it is as though the locale itself works to reverse this disjunction. Alive with motifs that circulate freely between above, below, within, and without, *sacred places reveal experiential glimpses of an "earthereal" future on a verdant globe where the human and the wild, and the built and the found, finally come back into balance as the witness becomes the witnessed.*

It is not anthropocentric to think of sacred places as magic mirrors, focusing elements, guides, teachers, and mentors. They approach us as emissaries, ambassadors, expert natural communicators to the degree they receive respect for what they are to themselves. Breakthroughs into deepening conversations with vibrant locations serve as acts of spiritual enlightenment. Every spiritual awakening not only blossoms in a particular place, it amplifies the sense of emplacement, of one's special place in a living world. The lowliest stone or mustard seed can ignite this epiphany of return, and send the bemused seeker home.

"In his passion and yearning," writes Stephanie Kaza about the puzzled Buddha at what is now Bodh Gaya in northeastern India, "he was called by a large fig tree to sit at its feet. This was the destination of his pilgrimage; he had come with his empty body and mind to receive great wisdom. He vowed not to move from the tree until he found the Great Truth."

He stared at the tree for a week, enraptured. And then:

For seven days and seven nights he sat in meditation, supported by the tree. During the seventh night he was tormented by every possible distraction of the mind. Mara, the voice of delusion, challenged him ferociously, asking what right he had to sit by the fig tree seeking the truth. To counter the force of ignorance, he touched his right hand to the earth. With the earth and tree as witness, the powerful realization of interdependence was revealed.[19]

"EVERYTHING IS FULL OF GODS"

"The Greeks learned about their Gods through unwritten mythology," notes James Hillman. "We learn about our archetypes through lived psychology."[20] We learn of their emplacement through reactive geography, until wider and wider vistas charged with aliveness and story, happenstance and dream, open up into cosmological possibilities.

Noting that the dramatist Aristophanes regarded bird oracles as the earliest religion, Susan Brind Morrow explains that our English word "nature" comes to us through Coptic from the early Egyptian *netcher* (god, sacred). It recalls the flags hung on poles planted over sacred places in the desert. "Five thousand years away there is an incidental pun: netcher equals nature."[21] The Ottomans named the tulip the Flower of God because the Arabic letters making up its name are those that spell Allah. In terms of geography, Giza for Ra, Ephesus for Artemis, Konohana Sakuya Hime on Mount Fuji, deities at the Ganges and the Gave de Pau River, residual double-faced energy in the walls and pillars of the Great Mosque in Cordoba: no sacred place stands devoid of the semi-autonomous presence of its resident *genius loci*.

Here, at last, after eons of keenly felt exile, we return with new tools and fresh ideas to reawaken from the ancestral past the question of whether *all archetypal powers everywhere, all perceptible configurations of the holy, wear the "inner" face whose outer form is place.*

To speak Greek for a moment, Artemis the Huntress, called Diana by the Romans, held sway in the wilderness. The impetuous hunter who spotted her there and ran home to brag was turned into a stag and eaten by his own hounds. Like Athena, goddess of city and culture, the unapproachable virgin Artemis was worshipped in a temple on the Acropolis, and also in Ephesus, the very city where a church council decided that Mary too was *chaste. Every unmanaged place around the globe preserves an Artemisian quality of untamed wildness.*

There is Aphrodite, born of sea foam, the great goddess of universal attraction from coagulations of quanta to galactic groupings; Nemesis, present in every forceful rebalancing; Dionysus, true brother to Artemis, but different in his love of city life; Hestia, divine glow of every hearth; Hephaestos, laboring away in every workshop; Poseidon, in wind, wave, and earthquake; and Zeus, the lightning-bearing sky-god, YHWH's Greek equivalent symbolized by the soaring eagle. Where would the guardian of the principle of far-seeing authority live but up in the heavenly heights?

The bonding of sacred presences to the structures of existence they animate holds whichever culture's deities we consider, descended Kuan Yin or ascended Parvati ("Mountain Dweller") or smiling Changing Woman, Navajo goddess of the Earth. The Aztec world associated Tezcatlipoca, the night god, with the north; Tlaloc, the rain god, with the south; Zipe Totec with sunrise in the east; and Quetzalcoatl, who visited the underworld, with the west. Add the intermediate points and witness the Lokapalas, the Guardians of the World in Hindu myth. *The cardinal directions speak like gods and these gods are cardinal directions.* The Zulu creator god Umvelinqangi appeared with the quakes and thunders. The liking of these deities for crags and valleys, surfaces and depths, abysses and peaks presses home the astonishing question of whether cosmological *kami* and the locales they frequent make two glowing windings in one immortal coil of divine immanence.

Continual encounters around the living world create an infinity of occasions to relocate oneself within an archetypalized cosmography where everything speaks within a measureless architecture of divinely balanced stresses. As in Welsh mythology, every earthly trek leads into the presence of the divine without raising much of a transitional din. The lock on the gate to Heaven's kingdom disappears, and the gate with it. "Olympus," Thoreau observed, "is but the outside of the earth everywhere."[22]

The relationship *between* these mythic figures is easily glimpsed at the local level. El Cajon, California, for example, whose name means "The Box" in Spanish, derives its name from the valley it sits in, where a layer of air keeps summers hot, like a lid placed over an oven. The motif of being boxed in recurs in squarish El Cajon's city history, from the tallest building in town (the jail) to the reactionary racism of local backwoods politics to Mount Helix, named after the box that a snail carries on its back. This metaphoric emphasis on confinement plays out within the garrisoned defendedness of San Diego County, which in turn comprises a westward-facing defense subsystem within the psyche of California. This 155,959-square-mile psyche also contains sectors or traits of activist idealism (San Francisco), craftsmanlike analysis (Alameda County), womblike fecundity (Silicon Valley, formerly the "Valley of Heart's Delight"), materialized projection (Los Angeles), creative depth (Monterey), learned beauty (Santa Barbara), recurrent ruptures (San Benito County), rushes of fancy (Santa Cruz), and other facets of geographized selfhood there on the psychic-geologic edge of the North American continent.

Millennia after it was uttered, before retreating to the margins, this simple statement, which Aristotle attributes to Thales, receives affirmation through a worldview that dares to be demonstrably animistic:

"Everything is full of gods."

And all of it, from Earth to the reaches of empty space to motes of dust to stellar nurseries to distant quasars still moving outward, all of it is evolving, alive, lined and limned with myth and dream-stuff after all, this mindfulness that birthed our own: animated, storied, growing, sentient, and nested in endless circles of influence as the soul-stuff of the universe arises from its tiniest emanations plucked from invisible strings. Whether pairs of particles arising out of hard vacuum, joining, and disappearing again, lands rising out of oceans, or newborn identities surfacing from unconsciousness, the cosmos resembles one seamlessly active psyche endlessly creative.

A *curious* species, we human beings, in both senses of the word. We listen through screens of loneliness for extraterrestrials without entertaining the suspicion that the interstellar immensities and the planet below might already be listening in on us.

"Beyond This Point…"

Until now maps have broken exploratory ground for roads, railways, cruciform power towers, steel-and-glass topsails leaning over future slums. The invaders come, see, buy, or steal, and as their pins proliferate and fresh explorations darken into highways, the presence of place, like the presence of the people who actually live there, suffers multiple levels of aching dismemberment.

> All the while, the living details of the place, the details that chronicle the daily intimacy of people with place—how they make their way, when the elk sip at the pool, where the tadpoles wriggle and grow, how the cottonwoods breathe into the wind— these details are missed and dismissed. They fall into oblivion, and only the details of the imperial fiat remain.[23]

But it does not have to be that way.

As these thoughts visit me at the shoreline, where I kneel to pick up a heart-shaped stone at continent's edge, I think about the history of my own conquered home, where I was born on the day Juan Cabrillo's sails appeared on the horizon. Story: the true stuff of interiority, for people and places alike. *I am the queen of a large seignory. … My lineage is very high, for my royal bloodline is so old there is no record of its beginning* …. So records Garcí Rodriguez de Montalvo's *The Exploits of Esplandian*, the first literary work to mention the name of California.[24] The invaders arrived not long after it was published. Cortez, Serra, Fremont come here yet, where they are not wanted, in the service of fiats still alien to the temper of this place. Nevertheless, the spirit of my homeland prevails unbroken. Long live the Queen.

Psychocartography, a recent piece of work against the human-nature rift, starts with an inventory of where a person dwells—the geography, the infrastructure, flora, fauna, gardens, neighborhoods, pathways, haunts, and, moving outward, permaculture zones, watersheds, bioregions—and deepens the information by tracing parallels between features of the environment and aspects of the inhabitant's psychology to link inner weeds with outer, cornerstones in many senses, flights of birds with flights of thoughts. The goal is to re-establish the broken sense of belonging to a place by getting to know it not only from the outside, but from the inside—its own and our own.

There is no need, however, for the pseudo-heroic go-it-alone that borrows from the posture of the empire-builders. The knowledge left in our cells and bones by a million years of earthly mutuality resurfaces in ecological face-to-face communities just as it always has. We carry our own coded instructions; all we need do is remember them in the kinds of encounters that call for them. Being at home in the world and with each other comes with the emplaced human form and requires surprisingly little to actualize its innate *participatory intelligence.*[25]

Better charts might help: charts of psyche and soil, myth and measurement, nomenclatures transparent to themselves. They might even help us understand the "inside story" of our own evolution: from one angle of view, a series of fortuitous mutations and natural selections, and from another, Terra/Gaia's perennial attempt to endow herself with consciousness, with ourselves as her musing bipedal spokespeople. Life: nature's doubling back on itself in elegances of complexity ever more refined. Seen in this interiorized way, evolution does not *create* subjectivity, it enriches and elaborates and focuses it through the hit-and-miss refinement of organs, tissues, and neural nets. With each turn of its spiral out of the alchemical *massa confusa* of nondifferentiation, the world grows more sensitive to itself as an inner-outer whole.

After several clumsy (because unconscious) protohuman attempts, things really moved forward 2.4 million years ago when gene MYH16 crossed itself a T, so to speak, and mutated to make room for smaller jaws, larger skulls. Two views, then, of one two-legged truth moving forward as an integrated whole as a differentiated consciousness dawned from primal darkness to wonder about itself and its place.

And about those who came before and did not make it, as we will not, should we fail to learn from our mistakes. "They came into being, they multiplied, they had daughters, they had sons, these manikins, woodcarvings," says the Mayan *Popul Vu* creation account about a previous race of humans. "But there was nothing in their hearts and nothing in their minds, no memory of their mason and builder. ... And so they fell, just an experiment and just a cutout for humankind."[26] Must we be a cutout for someone else?

Better charts might also trace a future worth extrapolating from those places we hold sacred because of the dreams they engender:

As the "Valhallic" technical/progressive/linear Fertile Crescent legacy rejoins its other "Nirvanic" half (the cultural/folkloric/metaphoric pole of the racial mind, which split off eleven thousand years ago), models of indigenous individuation blend scientific insights with earthy knowings. Nonsustainable empires fall from the maps; cities green from within; localized communities spring up like patches of growth in once-exhausted soil. Between and around them, roadways and highways give some ground back to those "blank" spots Aldo Leopold gently chastized us for failing to recognize as the most interesting on the chart.[27] All play a part in Terra's re-enchantment, human and non-human alike.

Bears are gone from the emergency rooms, and coyotes from the cities as the cities begin to shrink under skies now free of petrochemical darkness. Humane treatment of animals eliminates a source of raging pandemics. The lushness of self-regenerating watersheds overflow the scars of national borders, revealing these no man's lands to be as archaic as automobiles, oil rigs, or nuclear bows and arrows. A temblor catches no one at home; land-fitting buildings now constructed out of harm's way sway slightly and grow still. In the distance, a hurricane builds, changes its mind, and subsides into a restful, thirst-quenching rainstorm.

The ancient war against nature is finally over, and with it, the war of humans against humans. So much for the intractability of our nature.

Wherever it takes hold, and in whatever dialogical space of respect, appreciative love for the land redeems not only us, but Eden too, whose name means "delight," from her own ancient state of exile. For human beings working for a homecoming of all things, the water we swim in, the air we breathe, the ground we stand on, the sky above, our coming of age as a responsible species with unique obligations to self and place graces sacramental settings to which we know we belong.

Questions and Responses[†]

• *What motivated you to put together the terrapsychological approach?*

First came the need to understand my encounters with place, starting with the one mentioned in the Introduction: the dream in which San Diego appeared as a personified figure. In decades of work with dreams, nothing quite like that had ever happened to me. Gradually, I realized I was not alone in being addressed by the "voice" or presence of the land. I wrote this book to give my students and other "world therapists" and investigators of place something to start with if they need it, a framework for organizing ideas and impressions.

• *Was Kurt Lewin or other social scientists who study topology, proxemics, ergonomics, etc. much of an influence?*

Those disciplines were not designed to explore the subsurface connections I kept getting caught in, connections that spoke in image, metaphor, and repeating motifs we tend to share with the places where we live. The poets, naturalists, depth psychologists, and ecopsychologists were more helpful to me there. The pathways between us and where we visit and dwell can be traversed *literally*—sunlight correlated to certain moods, health

---

[†]Compiled from questions fielded by the author during interviews, classes, and presentations.

of habitat impacting human senses, the entire project of environmental and conservation psychology—but they are most deeply anchored in the experientially *thematic* soil ever-present behind the more linear conditions that symbolize it. As in other areas of human experience, symbolic resonances speak more richly and in more embodied tones than chains of causality can really tie down.

• *You have been presenting your terrapsychological work in different venues. How has it been received?*

Very favorably on the whole. People relate to having a deep attachment to particular places. Many have had dreams and encounters like the ones described in the book. I also hear from grateful people whose experiences with place or nature had been crammed back into their minds by well-meaning psychotherapists caught up in a paradigm that splits self from world.

• *Where did this reductive tendency in psychotherapy start?*

In psychotherapy, with Freud. For him, nothing is as it seems, and everything is a disguise for something else—for some less-than, or "nothing but," as William James put it. Even dreams censor themselves. "Defense," "superego," "stimulus barrier," "repression," and all those military images combine to make paranoid language, systematized suspicion, turning us ever inward, away from life. The field's real shadow entity is not lusty Eros, lover of union, it is distrustful Kronos, sickle-wielding fearer of rivals. Then there is its other side: relation, connection, contact. Freud reconnected psyche with body, and therefore with nature, and his emphasis on the transference paved the way for the psychoanalytic development of the transferential field.

• *There is a lot of blame heaped on Descartes for splitting self from world and mind from body.*

The fabric ripped long before Descartes. He just systematized the split. Perhaps we should see him more as a symptom of the cultural dissociation that still haunts us today than as a cause of it. Despite Descartes's enormous contribution—mathematics, Cartesian coordinates—there is an emotional deadness, and perhaps an envious cynicism, in its more positivistic manifestations.

• *Reduction of land experiences to the mother, or to the Great Mother, feels like a shrinking down of experience, doesn't it?*

A shrinkage, and a reversal. Reductionism makes the land symbolic of the personal; but, if anything, it is the other way around. I am a Californian. The reductive tendency would be to trace my edge-of-the-continent instincts to something in my family history and stop right there. But if you read about the history of this place, its presence as an edgy psychic being "west of the West" comes through clearly as a pattern extending over hundreds of years of recorded time. Geologically, the theme is even older. We who were born here have an instinctive feel for how to balance on shifting surfaces, but not only because of this or that in our upbringing. We do not "project" the liminal space of at-the-edge and in-between, we live in it. Sometimes we are it. It has always been that way for us.

• *How did you come up with the word "terrapsychology"?*

I was out walking and thinking about "locianalysis," which was the term I used in my dissertation to describe the method's use in talking about locations heavily wounded by human activity, and it occurred to me that I needed a wider term, something to describe a general approach to the presence of places both wounded and intact, and the word "terrapsychology" (TΨ) floated into my mind. The more I thought about it, the more sense it made. "Terra," the Roman word for the goddess of Earth, comes from a word meaning "dry land." In other words, it refers to places we have something to do with. This invokes a certain humility, this reminder that realms outside our ken remain mysterious. All in all, though, I am more concerned with listening to the surround than with what we call our efforts to do so. There is certainly no single way to go about it.

• *Do you regard terrapsychology as a subdivision of ecopsychology? Or the other way around?*

Psychologist Ralph Metzner has criticized what he sees as the departmentalizing of ecological perspectives, as though they could be confined to a specific school or campus wing. They need more room than that. So does TΨ. It is not a department, it is a way of studying and perceiving deep connections between people and places and things, one that embraces more surface-level disciplines, such as environmental psychology, without selling its soul to oppressive institutions.

• *What kinds of places have you studied?*

Neighborhoods, groves, deserts, mountains, suburbias, shorelines …. I began with California's Mission cities and their counties, examining the history, geography, ecology, politics, culture, architecture, etc. of each after spending enough time there for its presence to reach into my dreams, complexes, ecotransference. That would be 21 cities and 14 counties, not counting the surrounding cities, villages, parks, monuments, unincorporated areas, and so on. Then I studied Escondido and Phoenix, looked briefly in on Needles, and continued my tours throughout California. I am also interested in placefield motifs in prominent world cities, including New York, Paris, Moscow, Beijing, Cape Town, Athens, London, Tokyo, and Rome. I tend to get waylaid. As wetlands disappeared all over California, a breach in the Colorado River created the Salton Sea, as though by compensation, in the early 1900s. It is polluted now, but what potential still lurks in that enormous sink and stink? I wonder that every time I go by it.

• *Does any of this involve ordinary sightseeing?*

I think of it as "soulseeing." On a drive from Baltimore to Los Angeles I recorded some dreams and impressions along the way. I do that wherever I visit—places such as Judah Street in San Francisco, named after a railroad engineer pushed aside by greedy capitalists and "Silver Kings." Boosters named its district the Sunset to attract tourists and potential residents, who would be unaware of the frequent foggy gloom until after they disembarked. On certain streets the feel of the psychic undertow reminds me of nearby Ocean Beach. In the sea, regular rip currents, on land, the MUNI train carrying people away with tidelike regularity. Whether passing freighters or sidewalk sales, everything undulates together.

• *What criticisms of the work do you hear most often?*

The distancing, literal-minded kind—e.g., where are the laser-precise numbers? The controlled studies? This completely misses the point, of course. TΨ is not a quantitative theory about how the world works, it is a set of suggestions for making contact consciously. Do we expect "proof" from an instruction manual? The method was designed to help us tune into our inner relations with places and things while keeping an eye and ear on the outer ones, to counteract our tendency to fall into the tiresome de-animating habit of drowning out the inner by reducing it to the outer. The right tool for the right job! You cannot pick up a motif with a pair of tweezers, or confine the sound of the world to a laboratory. We tend to forget that all we know, objective or subjective, falls within the psychological field mentioned in the Introduction and therefore shares some of its dynamics.

• *Could Terrapsychological Inquiry be considered a form of qualitative research?*

Quasi-qualitative, perhaps. I prefer to think of it as carried out in an *intersubjective* space that includes both qualitative and quantitative forms of inquiry. The dividing up of research into two categories has tended to obscure the overarching intersubjective field in which all our efforts unfold.

• *In the chapter on archetypal geography you speak of myth as a living thing. What of the argument that myth is just an archaic form of discourse?*

The argument sounds postmodern, but it is actually premodern. Older in fact than Alcibiades of Athens, who mocked the gods shortly before the disastrous invasion of Syracuse. Down the centuries its name has shifted—atomism, euhemerism, Scholasticism, empiricism, positivism—but its campaign to conquer actually lived experience with rationality never varies. Myths can certainly be wielded defensively, but writing them off dogmatically as unreal or archaic hides a subordination of Reason to the hegemony of Procrustes.

• *Are there not states of consciousness beyond the realm of myth?*

States, perhaps, but places might well be another matter. What if myth is part of the landscape?

• *So, are the world and its places alive just because people dream they are, or intuit the aliveness, or have fantasies about it?*

A primary purpose of this research is to confirm whether dreams and intuitions and other "inner" promptings really echo local themes, details, woundings, vitalities, and histories, really describe something more than the insides of our heads. John Muir once remarked, beautifully, that by going out, he realized he was actually going in. It also works the other way around, you see, because our relations with the surround are interactive, they occur in one field. The more you let a place, a rock, a building, a broken bottle, a clean sweep of shoreline deeply into your psyche, the more animated it becomes. It gets into you as you get into it, and begins to reveal itself to you. It will not stand still any more. And a day comes when you realize with a start that a particular mood or propensity or turn of phrase of "yours" was inadvertently spoken in its own language.

• *How can one know how much of the "voice of place" is human projection?*

A similar issue comes up in psychotherapy: how do you know the client really displays a certain syndrome? Ultimately, you do not in any absolute sense, because both of you swim in the same interactive field, but being trained in detecting meaningful patterns helps as you pick up local images and movements and motifs, always keeping an eye on your weaknesses and having a sense of what you are liable to project. That is where feedback from other people becomes indispensable. Besides, projecting onto a place does not give the place presence or voice; it smothers both. Fortunately, the dialogical nature of the exploration tends to correct this. You cannot bury the local themes, stories, and traumas forever. The land will not permit it.

• *What is the most difficult thing to convey about actually doing terrapsychology?*

The power and urgency of being addressed directly by what you study. It is one thing to read a news story about a big snake that swallows an electric blanket a few days before the nation is swept by a record heat wave probably driven by global warming, or about a marlin spearing a fisherman off the coast of overfished Bermuda—do these events mean anything? Who knows? —but quite another to suffer the intensity of ecological transference impacting your moods or dreams or even choices of words. Places not only speak *to* us, they often speak *through* us. I think we should take a cue from psychoanalysis and start talking about ecological selfobjects: aspects of place whose jolting aliveness impinges on our own; or about the ecological equivalents of an operative family system.

• *Some would call such events synchronicities (symbolically meaningful coincidences).*

We are rethinking synchronicity as not so much an impersonal universal law as a gesture or a calling out. There are students now writing dissertations arguing that synchronicity is a kind of language or a conversation with the world.

• *A few times in the book you refer to places as "she." Do you equate the feminine with nature?*

No. I was speaking from experiences in which the presence of various locales would approach me in feminine form in dreams. I do not address the issue you raise because I do not feel qualified to. I am much more interested in what women have to say about it.

• *Archetypal psychologists tend to favor Plato, but you seem to like Aristotle. Why is this?*

Renaissance Neoplatonism unlocks a marvel of riches, but Plato gives me the shivers. His *Republic* in particular. George Orwell had a point when he wrote that otherworldliness and absolutism tend to go together. No one made a cult of Aristotle until the religious Scholastics watered him down. By contrast, I like Aristotle's image of the universe as a flow of becoming, moving from potentiality to actuality. I also like the fact that he held matter and Form (or Image, or Archetype) together rather than relegating the latter to a realm open only to Philosopher Kings. He does seem somewhat literal-minded at times, particularly when he restricts soul to the organic, but we have only his lecture notes to go by. He got passionate about mythology in his later years, but none of his work from that period survives. It would be interesting to see whether those studies modified his outlook.

• *But wasn't Jung rather otherworldly?*

In a Kantian sense, perhaps, and a Christian one too at times, but in his seminars you see him insisting again and again on remaining grounded in the here and now. On the whole, he avoided privileging the other world over this one.

125

• *In terms of this world, what do you think of some environmental extremists resorting to destruction of property to stop the builders and developers? What would the terrapsychological perspective say about them?*

Two things. First, these folks are marvelous scapegoats. Showing them being arrested on TV diverts attention from what big industry is doing to the planet. Never mind the oil barons overheating the atmosphere, get the guy who spikes a tree. However, whatever actions we take to protect what is left of the world should be rooted in simultaneous concern for nature, place, and each other. So we wonder if getting physically aggressive to protect a place demonstrates an overidentification with the pain of that place. It is like committing suicide on Earth Day. If I were Terra, I might be feeling somewhat suicidal too, but it helps no one if you drown in the same dark waters you are trying to haul someone out of.

• *We are so used to seeing things such as hurricanes as merely physical manifestations that it is difficult to switch lenses and see them as simultaneously ensouled. Is it really possible to hold both views?*

Think of a person protesting an injustice, or even an animal instinctively biting a tormentor. From the outside, we see a mass of muscles and neurochemistry; from the inside, the way animism, dream, and myth view it, a kind of undifferentiated but evident intentionality. Taken together as an amalgam: a *personality*. A place taken together, regarded as a whole, is a *presence*. Holding a hurricane like this, we can give it back its liveliness while resisting the impulse to explain away its most tragic effects.

• *The description of humanity as a kind of blight or disease on Terra's face loses sight of the human cost.*

Quite. It is misanthropic. Beyond that, it is just a surface greening of the old punishment paradigm. Instead of a sky god, it is now the angry earth mom beating us up for our sins—guilty and innocent alike. But storms and earthquakes do not care who gets hurt. It takes a highly differentiated, evolved, and perhaps mortal subjectivity to feel hatred or compassion as we understand them. Or to lack compassion. Look at depressed New Orleans, still hurting—and more than a year after Katrina, that devastating offspring of global warming.

126

• *It is strange to think of a place or an object as a kind of reactive entity.*

Our dualistic habit of seeing consciousness as an on/off either/or does not help. It takes a bit of imagination to see, say, an ecosystem as a kind of rudimentary nervous system, and to bear in mind that cognitive operations are prefigured and paralleled in the world around us. One value of Teilhard de Chardin's work is that he got us thinking about consciousness as a continuum, a quality rather than a thing that some beings have and others do not.

• *How is looking for an unconscious aliveness or "intent" in nature different from, say, Creationism?*

Comparing them would be like saying indigenous animistic thinking is a form of Creationism. It is not. (When Creationism was renamed "ID," for "Intelligent Design," I actually thought at first that someone was invoking Freud, as in ego, superego, and ID.) The real issue is not that some people believe in the divine creation or animation of the world; there are evolutionists who believe that too. The overwhelming majority of humans are spiritually inclined, and so is at least one terrapsychologist. The real issue is theocratic authoritarianism versus freedom of life and thought. Making the wrong choice is likely in the end to prove Darwin definitively right.

• *So is the terrapsychological perspective a spiritual perspective?*

It is for me. Spirituality: engaged, ongoing participation in and awe of the world's kaleidoscopic daimonisms.

• *Of course, scientists have been saying for years that Creationism is nonsense.*

Yes, but without offering any alternative view but that of a safely dead planet shaken by mindless, random forces. Such a picture is discouraging and invalidating to sensitive people whose intuition tells them otherwise.

• *What do you think of the idea of coming in and somehow "clearing" a wounded place of "negative energy"?*

I am not an expert on all the work done in this direction, so I will confine myself to what I see as its shadow side: the quick-fix mentality we also see in therapy fads that purport to erase a lifetime of emotional trauma by making the client ingest a pill or move his or her eyes this way or that. I think this "make it go away" mentality is one reason why it never seems actually to go away. Native Americans call this sort of thing "plastic shamanism." There is no magic wand or technique I know of for repairing decades—or in the case of the land, centuries—of trauma. My interest is in getting to know a place: its injuries, its deep past, what it has to say about itself, not in barging in and trying to fix it according to my standards of healing. I never know what a place needs until I allow its features, wounds, and spirit into me, and sometimes not even then. Who am I to say what it should lose or get over?

• *How has terrapsychological work changed you?*

I spent most of my youth feeling like an orphan in my own homeland. Not any more. I feel like I belong here. I live awash in an interactive mood in which aspects of the world feel like internalized parts of me, Californian parts in particular, and vice versa. For instance, when I feel I should be on guard, I do not consult an inner defense system, I ask myself: how does my San Diego side feel about this? Or, is my Sonoma West County side urging me to transcend the situation spiritually? Likewise, places I have come to know do not feel like lines on maps any more: they feel like persons. What harms or helps Los Angeles harms or helps me. It always did; but now I am aware of it. My heart is not just a pump in the chest any more, it is an emotional analog or hologram of what goes on in the world. As I tell my depth psych students, the heart is a nexus where introversion and extraversion can alternate in a heartbeat. My heart informs me that the world does not belong to me: I belong to it. I know my place.

• *What are your hopes for terrapsychology?*

Given how it started, TΨ has already accomplished its primary purpose: to encourage listening *in* on places, things, landscapes, animate objects. Anything else is a plus. Perhaps for some the framework can serve as a kind of instrument for playing an ecopsychological melody or two between human ears and stirring locales. That would be nice. I sometimes listened to a Bach fugue while tuning it.

• *A very musical image.*

Brahms was right—"In the beginning was Rhythm"; and I suspect he knew it because Terra whispered it into his soul, over and over, until he could finally vocalize it.

• *What do you mean by Valhallic and Nirvanic tendencies in the collective psyche?*

It is shorthand for addressing a split that began with a global climate shift 11,000 years ago, when some of us began focusing on agriculture, individualism, and abstract thought while others focused more on the enrichment of story, folklore, and relationship. It is a mistake to think that one group stagnated while the other progressed, or that neither bears anything of the other within it. What makes our time in history unique is that these two great traditions, schemas, and styles of living, finally fully developed, now seek ways to come back together ("Terrania"?) without one having to dominate the other. It is like some vast, evolutionary experiment coming to fruition. Will it succeed, or will we end up in the hominid version of an archeological cul-de-sac? The outcome is up to us.

• *Do you mean that one segment of humanity went one way and the other went another?*

Nothing so literal. One could perhaps talk about predominantly Valhallic cultures (the United States, for example), or primarily Nirvanic, but every group of people carries both poles. Every person, in fact. They are social-psychic tendencies in the species as a whole, a sort of long-term division of developmental labor pushing to bring about a reunion of intricately worked out rootedness, tradition, and mythopoesis with equally evolved individualism and know-how. It will require consciousness, however, to make the marriage work.

• *What could the goal of this be?*

Fully human beings at home in the world we delight in, tend, and turn gently to account. Fuller responsibility taken for serving as a kind of ego-consciousness of the planetary psyche. A partnership of wise interdependency rather than overidentification or domination. A mature relationship to place and planet, to ourselves and each other.

• *Does this mean you see a necessity in centuries of conquest, destructive industrialization, and the extinction of primal cultures? By valuing technics, aren't you also valuing their darkest consequences?*

No, and no. Spaniards did not conquer the New World because they liked to play with gunpowder and swords, believed they held a divine mandate, or needed "differentiation from the Feminine," but because their conquistadors were sent forth from an exhausted nation gutted by centuries of religious warfare, intolerance, and extermination at the hands of emotionally immature "leaders" afraid of nature, science, and technology. The fact that a development is one-sided or otherwise destructive (see Chapter 1) does not mean the original impulse is. Wrecking a civilization through pollution or greed is not at all the same as wanting to construct a pocket knife, concoct a new alloy, or look at the heavens through a telescope. When science is co-opted by destructive strivings, we need to analyze the strivings rather than succumb to the Manichean temptation to treat science as either devil or redeemer. We need to look at why our technics feed off the world instead of rejuvenating and nourishing it. It does not have to be this way.

• *Name one wondrous thing post-Fertile Crescent development brought to the table of human wholeness that was not there before.*

Seeing Earth, our home, from space, hanging out there in the alien void like a shining, fragile jewel. This grand vision changed forever our view of ourselves, our planet, and our place in the universe. I often wonder what Earth made of it. Spaceborne cameras as Gaia's hand mirrors.

• *What might be the political implications of living in an inter-animistic world?*

If spreading planetary wastelands parallel desertification of psyche and soul, then politics and community work will have to take place into account as a fully reactive participant. Air, sea, animal, insect, and land sit at the table with us. They are the table. Will we recognize them? We must. We must also replace divisive, immature, and paranoid politicians with wise elders: women and men who can interpret the language of the world, facilitate dialogical awareness, and speak in the tones of the elements while preserving maximum human complexity. In our day, this reweaving of the sacred fabric of place, spirit, society, self, and heart—in other words, deep heartsteading—includes recognizing clearly that it is not about sustainability any more or recycling a bit of aluminum. It is about staying alive. And what good is surviving if we do not survive whole?

• *In one sentence: if* **anima mundi***, or Gaia, or Terra, is reactively furious with us, what should we do to end the war?*

"Nature turns toward us the face that we turn toward it."

• *Do you think we are capable of destroying the world?*

No. We *are* destroying large sectors of the ecosphere, but it is an argument that Terra will eventually win as she moves to rebalance herself. My fear is that we will prove too Valhallically arrogant and inflexible— too one-sided—to survive the rebalancing; that we will go the way of the tens of thousands of species now dying off; and that the fall of empire so evident all around might drag down what is valuable along with it. But we need not worry about having the final word. As Gary Snyder said in a talk he gave years ago, "Nature bats last."

Notes

CHAPTER 1

1. R. Brian Ferguson, "10,000 Years of Tribal Warfare: History, Science, Ideology and 'The State of Nature,'" *The Journal of the International Institute* 8.3 (Spring/Summer 2001), http://www.umich.edu/~iinet/journal/vol8no3/ferguson.html (accessed January 25, 2005).

2. Calvin Clawson, *Mathematical Mysteries: The Beauty and Magic of Numbers* (New York and London: Plenum Press, 1996).

3. Jared Diamond, *Guns, Germs, and Steel: The Fate of Human Societies* (New York: W. W. Norton, 1999).

4. *Ibid.*

5. Richard Tarnas, *Cosmos and Psyche: Intimations of a New World View* (New York: Viking, 2006). Tarnas refers to these two attitudes—the colossal-mistake view of history and the progressive-idealization view—as "Edenic" and "Promethean."

6. Diamond, 410.

7. In his notebooks, Nietzsche put it thus: "How did the exhausted come to make the laws about values? Put differently: How did those come to power who are the last?—How did the instinct of the human animal come to stand on its head?" Friedrich Nietzsche, *The Will to Power*, ed. and trans. Walter Kaufmann (New York: Vintage, 1968), 34.

8. Dick Teresi, *Lost Discoveries: The Ancient Roots of Modern Science—From the Babylonians to the Maya* (New York: Simon & Schuster, 2002).

9. Interesting intuitions and foreshadowings sometimes surface even in madness. Today, the world supply of petroleum is beginning to reach peak as nipple-shaped wells continue to drain it from the ground. Will we take steps toward energy emancipation or wait until the breast runs dry?

10. Edward S. Casey, *Getting Back into Place: Toward a Renewed Understanding of the Place-World* (Bloomington, IN: Indiana University Press, 1993).

11. Albert Camus, *The Rebel: An Essay on Man in Revolt* (New York: Vintage, 1991).

12. Alun Munslow, *Deconstructing History* (London: Routledge, 1997), 15.

13. Laura Mitchell, *The Eco-Imaginal Underpinnings of Community Identity in Harmony Grove Valley: Unbinding the Ecological Imagination*, unpublished doctoral dissertation, Pacifica Graduate Institute, 2005, 105-06.

14. W. Scott Olsen and Scott Cairns, eds., *The Sacred Place: Witnessing the Holy in the Physical World* (Salt Lake City, UT: University of Utah Press, 1999), 151.

CHAPTER 2

1. Onno van der Hart and Klees van der Velden, "The Hypnotherapy of Andries Hoek: Uncovering Hypnotherapy before Janet, Breuer, and Freud," *American Journal of Clinical Hypnosis*, 4 (April 29, 1987): 264-71. Dr. Van der Hart believes "Rika van B" to be the client's real name in shortened form (personal communication, 2006).

2. Henri Ellenberger, *The Discovery of the Unconscious: The History and Evolution of Dynamic Psychiatry* (New York: Basic Books, 1970).

3. Heinz Ansbacher and Rowena Ansbacher, *The Individual Psychology of Alfred Adler* (New York: Harper Perennial, 1964).

4. For a collection of examples of this aspect of Jung's thought, see C. G. Jung, *The Earth Has a Soul: The Nature Writings of C. G. Jung*, ed. Meredith Sabini (Berkeley, CA: North Atlantic Books, 2002).

5. Arne Naess and David Rothenberg, eds., *Ecology, Community, and Lifestyle: Outline of an Ecosophy* (New York: Cambridge University Press, 1990).

6. Thomas Berry, *The Dream of the Earth* (San Francisco, CA: Sierra Club Books, 1990).

7. Kirkpatrick Sale, *Dwellers in the Land: The Bioregional Vision* (Athens, GA: University of Georgia Press, 2000).

8. Chellis Glendinning, personal communication, 2004.

9. Chellis Glendinning, *My Name is Chellis, and I'm in Recovery from Western Civilization* (Boston, MA: Shambhala, 1994).

10. Vandana Shiva, *Staying Alive: Women, Ecology, and Survival in India* (New York: St. Martin's Press, 1989).

11. Jerry Mander, *In the Absence of the Sacred: The Failure of Technology & the Survival of the Indian Nations* (San Francisco, CA: Sierra Club Books, 1991).

12. Theodore Roszak, Mary Gomes, and Allen Kanner, eds., *Ecopsychology: Restoring the Earth, Healing the Mind* (Berkeley, CA: University of California Press, 1995), 240.

13. David Orr, *Ecological Literacy: Education and the Transition to a Postmodern World* (New York: State University of New York Press, 1991).

14. Robert Greenway, personal communication, 2004.

15. Theodore Roszak, *The Voice of the Earth: An Exploration of Ecopsychology* (Grand Rapids, MI: Phanes Press, 1992), 14.

16. James Hillman and Michael Ventura, *We've Had a Hundred Years of Psychotherapy, and the World's Getting Worse* (San Francisco, CA: HarperSanFrancisco, 1992), 5.

17. Due to incidents of road rage, the psychology industry has recently been describing the frequency of Intermittent Explosive Disorder as underestimated—without saying a word about worsening congestion, lengthier driving times, the skyrocketing price of gasoline, the frustration of watching its suppliers making record profits, wars fought for oil, shame at having to add pollution to the sky, or anything else going on outside the IE (Identified Exploder).

18. Andy Fisher, *Radical Ecopsychology: Psychology in the Service of Life* (New York: State University of New York Press, 2002).

19. Roszak, *et al.*, xvi.

20. Definition jointly designed by Robert Greenway, Amy Lenzo, Gene Dilworth, Robert Worcester, and Linda Buzzell-Saltzman.

21. Fisher, 22.

22. Paul Shepard, *Nature and Madness* (Athens, GA: University of Georgia Press, 1998).

23. Roszak, *et al.*, 116.

24. Catherine Roach, *Mother/Nature: Popular Culture and Environmental Ethics* (Bloomington, IN: Indiana University Press, 2003).

25. James Hillman, Lecture at Pacifica Graduate Institute, 2004.

Chapter 3

1. Keith Basso, *Wisdom Sits in Places: Landscape and Language among the Western Apache* (Albuquerque, NM: University of New Mexico Press, 1996).

2. Marie-Louise von Franz, *Alchemical Active Imagination* (Boston, MA: Shambhala, 1997).

3. Arthur Schopenhauer, *The World as Will and Representation, Vol. I*, trans. E. F. J. Payne (New York: Dover, 1969).

4. Baruch Spinoza, *The Ethics, Treatise on the Emendation of the Intellect, and Selected Letters*, trans. Samuel Shirley; ed. and intro. Seymour Feldman (Indianapolis, IN: Hackett, 1992).

5. Pierre Teilhard de Chardin, *The Phenomenon of Man*, trans. Bernard Wall (New York: Perennial, 1976).

6. William Seager, "Panpsychism," *Stanford Encyclopedia of Philosophy*, 2001, http://plato.stanford.edu/entries/panpsychism/ (accessed September 15, 2003).

7. James Hillman, *Re-Visioning Psychology* (New York: Harper Perennial, 1976), 39.

8. Jung, *Earth Has a Soul*, 82.

9. C. G. Jung, *Psychology and Alchemy*, trans. R. F. C.Hull, Bollingen Series, vol. 12 (Princeton, NJ: Princeton University Press, 1968).

10. Karen Warren, ed., *Ecological Feminist Philosophies* (Bloomington, IN: Indiana University Press, 1996).

11. Val Plumwood, *Environmental Culture: The Ecological Crisis of Reason* (London: Routledge, 2002), 177.

12. Donald W. Winnicott, *Psycho-Analytic Explorations*, ed. Clare Winnicott, Ray Shepherd, and Madeleine Davis (Cambridge, MA: Harvard University Press, 1989), 559.

13. Joan and Neville Symington, *The Clinical Thinking of Wilfred Bion* (New York: Routledge, 1996).

14. Matthew Cochran is now working on what he has named *archetypal geology*. "One could say geologic behavior has a running engagement with psyche's movements" (personal communication, 2006).

CHAPTER 4

1. Craig Chalquist, "In the Shadow of Cross and Sword: Imagining a Psychoanalysis of Place," unpublished doctoral dissertation, Pacifica Graduate Institute, 2003.

2. Active association is a hybrid of free association (Freud)—something coming into the mind in response to a dream image—and active imagination, Jung's practice of entering a state of reverie to allow a fantasy image free play. Active association tends free associations, but only those that emanate directly from a particular image or event.

3. "Nomadic awareness" was a term coined simultaneously by Matthew Cochran and Laura Mitchell (2005).

4. John Mitchell, *Ceremonial Time: 15 Thousand Years on One Square Mile* (Cambridge: Perseus Books, 1984).

5. I have mentioned only a handful out of an abundance of local expressions of this Edenic theme.

6. Chalquist.

7. It is perhaps worth mentioning that while living in Sebastopol, I woke up one night with an intense but inexplicable pain in the ribs. In reference to the round birthmark on my right forearm, a dream repeated the nickname "Cain" before I left town.

8. Hillman, *Re-visioning Psychology*.

CHAPTER 5

1. Edward S. Casey, "Taking a Glance at the Environment: Prolegomena to an Ethics of the Environment," *Research in Phenomenology* 31 (2001): 8.

2. Joanna Macy, *World as Lover, World as Self* (Berkeley: Parallax, 1991).

3. Hillman, *Re-visioning Psychology*.

4. My thanks to Mary Watkins for helping me visualize psyche as an assembly of many voices in potential dialog with one another.

5. I mean "shamanic" in the indigenous sense, not the workshops/crayons/chanting sense that has colonized this once-useful word, particularly throughout the Bay Area, with self-development agendas quite unshamanic in character or aim. Possessed by commodification, self-development "shamanism" is itself in dire need of a shamanic ritual of soul-retrieval.

6. David Barnhill, ed., *At Home on the Earth: Becoming Native to Our Place: A Multicultural Anthology* (Berkeley, CA: University of California Press, 1999), 308-09.

7. Sigmund Freud, *Beyond the Pleasure Principle*, trans. James Strachey (New York: W. W. Norton, 1990).

8. There is a school of psychological thought that interpretive or diagnostic moves invariably obliterate the sense of direct experience. This need not happen when the phenomenological quality of encounter is tended first and subsequent interpretations are subordinated to it while maintaining their transparency as working fictions or fantasies.

9. "Terrapsychologizing" draws inspiration from what Hillman has named "psychologizing" or "seeing through" (*Re-visioning Psychology*) but focuses on the presence of a place or its features showing up behind/beyond/within the numbers and facts.

CHAPTER 6

1. Jane Wheelright Hollister and Linda Schmidt, *The Long Shore: A Psychological Experience of the Wilderness* (Collingdale, PA: Diane Publishing, 1991).

2. James A. Hall, *Jungian Dream Analysis: A Handbook of Theory and Practice* (Toronto: Inner City Books, 1988).

3. Jung, *Earth Has a Soul*.

4. Hillman, *Re-visioning Psychology*, xix.

5. *Ibid.*, iv.

6. Peter Ackroyd, *London: The Biography* (New York: Nan A. Talese, Doubleday, 2000), 552.

7. Theodore Roszak, *The Gendered Atom: Reflections on the Sexual Psychology of Science* (Berkeley: Conari Press, 1999).

8. Jung used the term "Complex Psychology" when referring to his work as a general psychology. See Sonu Shamdasani, *Jung and the Making of Modern Psychology: The Dream of a Science* (New York: Cambridge University Press, 2003).

9. C. G. Jung, *Psychological Types*, trans. R. F. C. Hull, Bollingen Series, vol. 6 (Princeton, NJ: Princeton University Press, 1971).

10. C. G. Jung, *Two Essays in Analytical Psychology*, trans. R. F. C. Hull, Bollingen Series, vol. 7 (Princeton. NJ: Princeton University Press, 1972).

11. C. G. Jung, *Alchemical Studies*, trans. R. F. C. Hull, Bollingen Series, vol. 13 (Princeton. NJ: Princeton University Press, 1968), 12.

12. Jung, *Psychological Types*, 187.

13. C. G. Jung, *Memories, Dreams, Reflections*, ed. Aniela Jaffé, trans. Richard and Clara Winston (New York: Vintage, 1965), 15; hereafter abbreviated to *MDR*.

14. Jung, *MDR*, 23.

15. C. G. Jung, *Structure and Dynamics of the Psyche,* trans. R. F. C. Hull, Bollingen Series, vol. 8 (Princeton, NJ: Princeton University Press, 1970).

16. Jung, *MDR*, 161.

17. *Ibid.*

18. *Ibid.*, 172.

19. This connection was suggested by Nancy Cater, personal communication, 2006.

20. Jung, *MDR*, 199.

21. *Ibid.*, 225-26.

22. Mary Shelley, *Frankenstein: or, The Modern Prometheus* (New York: Oxford University Press, 1998), 16.

23. Percy Shelley, *Prometheus Unbound* (Kila, MT: Kessinger, 2004), 35.

CHAPTER 7

1. Wolfgang Giegerich, "Closure and Setting Free, or the Bottled Spirit of Alchemy and Psychology," *Spring 74* (2006): 31-62.

2. Jung, *Alchemical Studies*, 91.

3. For an example see Robert Bosnak, "Sulphur Dreaming," *Spring 74* (2006): 91-106.

4. Jung, *Earth Has a Soul.*

5. Henri Bortoft, *The Wholeness of Nature: Goethe's Way toward a Science of Conscious Participation* (New York: Lindisfarne Press, 1996).

6. Jung, *MDR*, 205.

7. Marie-Louise von Franz, *Psyche and Matter* (Boston, MA: Shambhala, 1992), 145-46.

8. C. G. Jung, *Mysterium Coniunctionis*, trans. R. F. C. Hull, Bollingen Series, vol. 14 (Princeton, NJ: Princeton University Press, 1977), 525.

9. Jung, *Alchemical Studies*, 88.

10. H. Stanley Redgrove, *Alchemy, Ancient and Modern* (Kila, MT: Kessinger, 1921).

11. Saloman Trismosin and Adam McLean, eds., *Splendor Solis* (Grand Rapids, MI: Phanes, 1991), 21.

12. *Ibid.*

13. Jung, *Alchemical Studies*, 279.

14. *Ibid.*, 75.

15. *Ibid.*, 103.

16. *Ibid.*, 93.

17. *Ibid.*, 95.

18. Jung, *Mysterium Coniunctionis*, 297.

19. Trismosin and McLean, 89.

20. Pierre Teilhard de Chardin, *The Heart of Matter*, trans. Rene Hague (San Diego, CA: Harvest, 1976).

21. A. E. Waite, ed., *Collectanea Chemica: Being Certain Select Treatises on Alchemy and Hermetic Medicine* (Edmonds, WA: The Alchemical Press, 1991), 77.

22. Matthew Cochran, "The Eros of Erosion," unpublished paper, 2005.

23. Edward Edinger, *Anatomy of the Psyche* (La Salle, IL: Open Court, 1985).

24. Waite, 146-47.

CHAPTER 8

1. According to one online news report, evangelists had gotten busy interpreting Katrina as punishment for the sin of "unnatural" homosexuality in New Orleans. Naturally, there was no explanation offered as to why a homophobic God would create so many lifeforms whose members engage naturally in homosexual behavior. A few of them: birds, sheep, beetles, bats, penguins, dolphins, macaques, bonobos (some 75% of whom are thought to be bisexual), orangutans, and of course human beings. Punishment tends to be in the eye of the beholder.

2. Diamond.

3. "Preparing for the Unknowable: Why the Kashmir Earthquake Happened and What Might be Done," *The Economist*, October 13, 2005, http://www.economist.com/science/displayStory.cfm?story_id=5019727 (accessed November 15, 2005).

4. Sandip Roy, "A Mountain Tsunami in Kashmir," *AlterNet*, October 12, 2005, http://www.alternet.org/story/26711/ (accessed November 15, 2005).

5. "Mercy Holes in Wall of Control," *The Telegraph*, October 23, 2005, http://www.telegraphindia.com/1051023/asp/frontpage/story_5388677.asp (accessed November 15, 2005).

6. Bradford Hanson and Robert Bradley, "History of Oil & Gas in Louisiana and the Gulf Coast Region," *Black Gold Beneath the Bayous*, 1999, Louisiana State Department of Natural Resources, Louisiana State University, http://www.leeric.lsu.edu/bgbb/6/la_oil.html (accessed November 15, 2005).

7. Paul Rincon, "Faster Emergence for Diseases," *BBC News*, 2006, British Broadcasting Corporation, http://news.bbc.co.uk/2/hi/science/nature/4732924.stm (accessed February 20, 2006).

8. My thanks to Larry Robinson for this reminder that birds were used as auguries in Rome.

9. James Hillman, *The Thought of the Heart and the Soul of the World* (Dallas, TX: Spring, 1992), 97.

10. Andrew Martignoni, "Monks Mont: Retrospective and Prospective," unpublished Master's thesis, Southern Illinois University, December 12, 2003, http://www.siue.edu/CAHOKIAMOUNDS/Andy%20Thesis/index.htm (accessed January 25, 2005).

11. T. C. McLuhan, ed., *Cathedrals of the Spirit: The Message of Sacred Places* (New York: Harper Perennial, 1996), 174-75.

12. *Ibid.*, 33.

13. *Ibid.*, 217.

14. Olsen and Cairns, xiii.

15. Susan Brind Morrow, *The Names of Things: Life, Language, and Beginnings in the Egyptian Desert* (New York: Riverhead Books, 1999).

16. Benjamin Kedar and R. J. Werblowsky, eds., *Sacred Space: Shrine, City, Land* (New York: New York University Press, 1998).

17. *Ibid.*.

18. Olsen and Cairns, 141.

19. McLuhan, 220-21.

20. Hillman, *Re-visioning Psychology*, 36.

21. Morrow, 7.

22. Henry Thoreau, *Walden; or, Life in the Woods* (Boston, MA: Houghton Mifflin, 1995), 82.

23. Chellis Glendinning, *Off The Map: An Expedition Deep Into Empire and the Global Economy* (Gabriola Island: New Society Publishers, 2002), 20.

24. Garcí Rodriguez de Montalvo, *The Labors of the Very Brave Knight Esplandian*, trans. William Thomas Little (Binghamton, NY: Center for Medieval and Early Renaissance Studies, SUNY Binghamton, 1992).

25. Laura Mitchell.

26. Scott Leonard and Michael McClure, *Myth and Knowing*: *An Introduction to World Mythology* (New York: McGraw-Hill, 2004), p. 96.

27. Aldo Leopold, *A Sand County Almanac* (London: Oxford University Press, 1969).

Index

the future of 128
vs. spirituality 127
Texas 106
Tezcatlipoca 114
Thales 115
The Closing Circle (Commoner) 24
The Exploits of Esplandian (de
    Montalvo) 116
*The Sacred Place: Witnessing the Holy in
    the Physical World* (Olsen, Cairns)
    110
The Secret of the Golden Flower 92
The Unsettling of America (Berry) 30
The Voice of the Earth (Roszak) 33
theme(s) 4, 22, 49, 50, 55, 57, 58, 60–
    62, 65, 67, 68, 72, 123, 124
    Edenic 57
    historical 86
    in California 121
    in San Diego 4
    of ascent and descent 98
    place-embedded 59
    placefield 59
    Promethean, in Switzerland 78, 86
    self-storying 71
    Swiss 85, 86
    symptomatic 58
    that suggest trauma 62
Thoreau, Henry David 23, 24, 39, 51,
    114
Thus Spake Zarathustra (Nietzsche) 23
Tillich, Paul 81
Tlaloc 114
Tokagawa 23
Tokyo 122
Toller, Ernst 81
trauma 28, 49, 53, 54, 65, 71, 124, 128
    of place 4
    placefield 61

recurrent 62, 63
stories of 54
unanalyzed 2
Trickster 112
Trismosin, Salomon 97
tsunami 6, 55, 104

U

Umvelinqangi 114
unconsciousness 100, 104, 115
Ur-plant 94

V

Valhallic cultures 129
Valhallic orientation 117, 129, 131—*See
    also* Nirvanic orientation
van de Velde, Henri 81
van Gogh, Vincent 23
Ventura, Michael 33
Vizcaino, Captain Sebastián 2
voice of place 3, 4, 38, 49, 52, 65, 68,
    75, 119, 124
Voltaire 79
von Franz, Marie-Louise 45, 81, 95
von Hartmann, Eduard 46
von Laban, Rudolf 81
von Reventlow, Fanny 81
von Richthofen, Else 81

W

Wagner, Ricard 84
Walden (Thoreau) 24
warfare 11, 15, 16, 22, 25, 130
Warmouth, Art 32
*We've Had a Hundred Years of Psycho-
    therapy—And the World's Getting
    Worse* (Hillman, Ventura) 33
Wigman, Mary 81

SPRING JOURNAL BOOKS

The book publishing imprint of *Spring Journal*,
the oldest Jungian psychology journal in the world

STUDIES IN ARCHETYPAL PSYCHOLOGY SERIES
Series Editor: Greg Mogenson

Collected English Papers, Wolfgang Giegerich
  Vol. 1: *The Neurosis of Psychology: Primary Papers Towards a Critical Psychology*, ISBN 1-882670-42-6, 284 pp., $20.00
  Vol. 2: *Technology and the Soul*, ISBN 1-882670-43-4
  Vol. 3: *Soul-Violence* ISBN 1-882670-44-2
  Vol. 4: *The Soul Always Thinks* ISBN 1-882670-45-0

Dialectics & Analytical Psychology: The El Capitan Canyon Seminar, Wolfgang Giegerich, David L. Miller, and Greg Mogenson, ISBN 1-882670-92-2, 136 pp., $20.00

Northern Gnosis: Thor, Baldr, and the Volsungs in the Thought of Freud and Jung, Greg Mogenson, ISBN 1-882670-90-6, 140 pp., $20.00

Raids on the Unthinkable: Freudian and Jungian Psychoanalyses, Paul Kugler, ISBN 1-882670-91-4, 160 pp., $20.00

The Wounded Researcher: A Depth Psychological Approach to Research, Robert Romanyshyn, ISBN 1-882670-47-7

The Sunken Quest, the Wasted Fisher, the Pregnant Fish: Postmodern Reflections on Depth Psychology, Ronald Schenk, ISBN: 1-882670-48-5, $20.00

Fire in the Stone: The Alchemy of Desire, Stanton Marlan, ed., ISBN 1-882670-49-3, 206 pp., $22.95

Honoring David L. Miller

Disturbances in the Field: Essays in Honor of David L. Miller, Christine Downing, ed., ISBN 1-882670-37-X, 318 pp., $23.95

The David L. Miller Trilogy

Three Faces of God: Traces of the Trinity in Literature and Life, David L. Miller, ISBN 1-882670-94-9, 197 pp., $20.00

Christs: Meditations on Archetypal Images in Christian Theology, David L. Miller, ISBN 1-882670-93-0, 249 pp., $20.00

Hells and Holy Ghosts: A Theopoetics of Christian Belief, David L. Miller, ISBN 1-882670-99-3, 238 pp., $20.00

The Electra Series

Electra: Tracing a Feminine Myth through the Western Imagination, Nancy Cater, ISBN 1-882670-98-1, 137 pp., $20.00

Fathers' Daughters: Breaking the Ties That Bind, Maureen Murdock, ISBN 1-882670-31-0, 258 pp., $20.00

Daughters of Saturn: From Father's Daughter to Creative Woman, Patricia Reis, ISBN 1-882670-32-9, 361 pp., $23.95

Women's Mysteries: Twoard a Poetics of Gender, Christine Downing, ISBN 1-882670-99-XX, 237 pp., $20.00

Gods in Our Midst: Mythological Images of the Masculine—A Woman's View, Christine Downing, ISBN 1-882670-28-0, 152 pp., $20.00

Journey through Menopause: A Personal Rite of Passage, Christine Downing, ISBN 1-882670-33-7, 172 pp., $20.00

Portrait of the Blue Lady: The Character of Melancholy, Lyn Cowan, ISBN 1-882670-96-5, 314 pp., $23.95
